THE BENEDICTINE WAY

The Benedictine Way

Wulstan Mork, OSB

WIPF & STOCK · Eugene, Oregon

Wipf and Stock Publishers
199 W 8th Ave, Suite 3
Eugene, OR 97401

The Benedictine Way
By Mork, Wulstan
Copyright © 1987 by Mork, Wulstan All rights reserved.
Softcover ISBN-13: 978-1-6667-5120-8
Hardcover ISBN-13: 978-1-6667-5121-5
eBook ISBN-13: 978-1-6667-5122-2
Publication date 6/16/2022
Previously published by St. Bede's Publications, 1987

This edition is a scanned facsimile of the original edition published in 1987.

Imprimi potest: David J. Cyr, OSB
Abbot

Nihil obstat: Charles W. McNamee, S.T.L., J.C.L.
Censor deputatus

Imprimatur: Arthur J. O'Neill
Bishop of Rockford
21 January 1987

The *Nihil obstat* and *Imprimatur* are official declarations that a book or pamphlet is considered to be free of doctrinal and moral error. It is not implied that those who have granted the *Nihil obstat* or *Imprimatur* necessarily agree with the contents, opinions, or statements expressed.

Acknowledgment

Quotations from *RB 1980* (copyright © 1980 by The Order of St. Benedict, Inc., published by The Liturgical Press, Collegeville, MN) are used with permission.

Contents

Introduction

The Benedictine Way is a mentality. It is true, the monastic life has definite elements that existed before St. Benedict and that have come down to his followers in and by means of his Rule. But in the long run what emerges is an attitude, or a set of attitudes, and it is this viewpoint that distinguishes the Benedictine monk and nun, as it provides their *via vitae* (*RB*, Prologue).

I am using *way* here basically as a road. A road has a destination, and people use it to reach a certain place. (I'm not concerned with those drivers who are only "out for a ride," to enjoy the scenery.) As such, a road is a means to get to an End. *Way* can also mean *method* and *manner*—which are really roads—and the Benedictine Way would include these meanings too. However, Benedictines don't quite like methods in their spiritual life, so I shall substitute the word *elements* instead. *Order* is an acceptable near-synonym.

What is the destination of the Benedictine Way? It is that of all Christians—the eternal life that Christ came to merit and give, the experience of the Father and the Son, by their love, the Holy Spirit (cf. Jn. 17:3). This is the "city" to which the Benedictine Way goes, the *Urbs Jerusalem Beata*. But the Benedictine strives to reach this city before he actually gets there, and he hopes to stop and sojourn in its outer reaches before God eternally lets him in the city gate. As is the case with every metropolis, there are suburbs. Driving through these, the eager driver knows that he's getting there. But then there are bleak stretches of open country, which only make him hurry on to his destination.

Leaving this metaphor of a road to a city, I would like to introduce the *elements* that are an essential part of the Benedictine Way. (The metaphor-lovers can, I am sure, fit these in neatly.) They are: continual prayer, *lectio divina,* the common life, the *Opus Dei,* the specifically Benedictine vows of obedience, stability, and *conversatio morum,* separation from the world, and work. These elements are means, and necessary means, and they cannot be rejected or rationalized away.

Some individuals feel that the various works our monasteries are doing—call them "apostolic" works—are out of place for Benedictines. They envision an authentic Benedictine monastery as one that has no school and whose priest-monks do not go out for specifically priestly activities, particularly the care of parishes. Some others believe that the monks must "trim down" the monastic elements because of the nature and pressure of their monastery's works. Still others see Benedict's charism as something that can't yet be defined, and regard his spirituality as being still in process.

My thesis in this book is that a Benedictine monastery must keep the elements of Benedictine monastic life because they are essential to the Benedictine Way. If a monastery is faithful to these elements, the monks will acquire a mentality that will enable them to view everything from the standpoint of their destination, their End. If anyone were to stop a monk during the day and ask him, "What are you doing?" his first thought would not be, "I am teaching a class," but either "I am going to God," or even "I am united with God." His mentality will never let him take an interesting detour to another destination as he pursues his way. In fact the true Benedictine mentality will impel him to go out to others to bring them with him in his search for God, or to share the God whom he has found.

A charism is a grace that God gives a person for the good of the Church. St. Benedict's charism is the grace to make the elements of Eastern monasticism adaptable and available to the West. It's up to the monk or nun to adapt to these elements. Therein lies the process.

The Benedictine Way can be used as a basis for the formation of novices. It can also provide the material for renewal, for re-formation. It is simply a return to St. Benedict's sources, to what our tradition has done with these sources, as well as a consideration of what our own generation of monks and nuns is doing with them and can do. To quote Abbot John Chapman's maxim, *solvitur ambulando*—it all becomes clear as we go along the Benedictine Way.

While the book was intended originally for Benedictines—an "inside" book—various readers have suggested that it be published and made available to others. After all, behind Western civilization is the Rule of St. Benedict. And the same Rule influenced the formation of the later religious Orders and Congregations. These religious today are beginning to realize that the word *monastic* isn't always a wrong word for them, and are searching for ancient ways of praying that are definitely monastic.

People today have a great hunger for prayer and want instruction about how to pray. The Benedictine way of prayer is simple and direct and comes from the men and women who lived with God in the Egyptian desert, who sought and found him.

The laity want to return to the sources of Christian spirituality and can easily appreciate the Benedictine Way. Many lay people are and have been for centuries affiliated spiritually with Benedictine monasteries as oblates, basing their lives in the married and single states on the Rule of St. Benedict.

St. Benedict wrote his Rule originally for men, and since I am commenting upon this Rule I usually refer to monks. Often one can write "monks and nuns," but then later in the sentence there can occur "his or her," "him and her," and this becomes quite distracting. Actually, in the light of the fact that women have followed the Rule from the beginning, the use of "monk" in the Rule has been understood generically, to mean both men and women. It is in this sense that I use it. Our lay-oblates have had no trouble in making the adjustment of the word to refer to anyone who wishes to follow the Rule. The Rule has a universal appeal, and I want *The Benedictine Way* to make that appeal available to all.

Abbot David J. Cyr's enthusiasm for this book and constant interest in it, together with his blessing which made the writing of it part of my work, have helped me through it as a means of grace. My dedication of the book to him will let him know my recognition of his part in it.

My confrere, Brother Leander Hogg, prepared the manuscript for private distribution with his quiet monastic selflessness. His good advice has always sprung from his own sound Benedictine mentality.

Marmion Abbey,
Aurora, Illinois

THE BENEDICTINE WAY

I

Monks Have Only One End

A PERSON BECOMES A BENEDICTINE for only one purpose, to seek union with God. He may be a professional, a craftsman, or a student with a special intellectual interest. The monastery he is entering may have an excellent school. But he comes there looking for God. What God does with his talents and accomplishments is totally immaterial to him: he wants God alone. And the monastery is interested in only one thing: is the person seeking God alone.

This may seem contrary to appearances and even to actual cases. A person may certainly enter a Benedictine monastery that has a school because he wants to teach, but it is the business of the novice master to "straighten him out," to show him that teaching is not of the essence of Benedictine life, that the Benedictine novice has to have only one objective, and to determine during the course of the novitiate whether his sole objective is seeking union with God. If he persists in expecting that his working life is going to be spent in the classroom, he is told to apply to a religious community that has been founded for teaching.

Monks and nuns have only one end or purpose and this fact distinguishes them from what the Church calls "religious," who have at least two ends. Religious Orders and Congregations have all been founded to take care of some need in the Church; they all have definite works to do that flow from their particular spirit. Their primary end is, of course, union with God and the growth of their members in Christian holiness, but they always have a secondary end, e.g., the Dominicans were founded to preach; the Jesuits, to serve the Church in any needed capacity. (There are Orders and Congregations of cloistered Sisters who have a "monastic" character because they have only the one end, union with God.)

So if a person believes God is calling him to serve the sick, preach parish renewals, do pastoral or social work, or teach, he enters an Order or Congregation whose secondary purpose is to perform these works, and in which he can have the reasonable assurance that he will perform them. If he believes that God is calling him simply to seek Him, and, finding Him, to live intimately with Him, he enters an Order of monks.

There are four main Orders of monks in the Church: the Benedictines, the Cistercians, the Carthusians, and the Camaldolese. Actually there are two Orders of Cistercians: the Common Observance and the Strict Observance or Trappists. There are also two Orders of Camaldolese: the original Order and a reform group, the Camaldolese Hermits of Monte Corona. All of these Orders, except the Carthusians, follow the Rule of St. Benedict. The original Order of Camaldolese was taken into the Benedictine Confederation in 1966.

Monks are heirs of the Desert Fathers, those men (and women too—Desert Mothers) who poured into the Egyptian deserts and hills to seek God alone in solitude and renunciation. Later they went to deserted places in other countries of the Middle East. They were called in Greek *monachoi,* from the word *monos,* which means *alone, solitary.* So a *monachos* was one who fled from the world to seek God alone in solitude and isolation from all temptations and distractions. Even when St. Pachomius organized into communities those who wanted to leave the world and seek God, the members were still called *monachoi* because they were doing what the word denoted.

When St. Athanasius, the archbishop of Alexandria, was exiled to Rome in 340, he told an eager audience about what his friend, St. Anthony, and the other Egyptian monks were doing. Tradition has it that he was accompanied by two monks who were disciples of St. Anthony. That visit, and St. Athanasius' life of St. Anthony, which he wrote after that great monk's death, had a tremendous influence on the spread of the monastic way of life in Europe. St. Martin of Tours began an Egyptian-style community of hermits at Ligu   é in 361 and another near Tours when he became bishop of that city.

By the time John Cassian came to Marseilles in the early 400s, the monastic life was an established institution in the Western Church, although floundering for lack of solid guidance. Cassian wrote his *Institutes* and *Conferences* to supply that guidance, to give detailed information about organizing a monastery, and to teach monks and nuns and their novices the spirituality of the Egyptian Desert Fathers.

When St. Benedict began his monastery at Monte Cassino it was merely one out of many monasteries. He was by no means bringing something new to Europe. What he brought was his Rule, which wasn't exactly new in much of its material. It leaned heavily on the rule of another Italian monastery, the *Rule of the Master,* which, in turn, borrowed from Cassian, as did St. Benedict.

St. Benedict's Rule became popular because it was a workable rule—practical and balanced. It was not too detailed but left much to the abbot and community. Part of its practicality was due to its adaptability. But it was a rule for monks, and monks in the Egyptian tradition. St. Benedict was simply doing for an Italian monastery what Cassian did for European monastic life in general—adapt for time and place the principles and practices of the Desert Fathers.

So we are back where we started in the first paragraph of this chapter. A Benedictine is a monk (or nun) in the technical sense of that word. His monastery may have a school, and he may spend most of his life teaching in it. The monastery may have some parishes, and he might devote years to pastoral work. Some individuals may work in specialized ministries, but these apostolic and humanitarian works are not of the essence of Benedictine life.

An abbey can close its school or give it to seculars, a diocese can take over Benedictine parishes, and the life of the abbey goes on. We are familiar with Catholic high schools, once owned and taught by a religious Order or Congregation, that have closed. The religious leave also and are reassigned to other houses of their Institute because their reason for being there no longer exists. Not so with Benedictines. Their reason for being there is eternal. Their occupations may come and go but Benedictines remain, seeking God through other means.

The fact that Benedictines have only one end has not always been stated in so many words. Abbot Butler put it simply as leading "the monastic life according to the Rule of our Holy Father Benedict."[1]

In the old Declarations and Constitutions of the two American Congregations of Benedictine monks, the idea of the one end was there but not formulated as such. The Declarations of the Swiss-American Congregation of 1955 could state: "The primary aim of our Congregation is none other than the one proposed in the Holy Rule of our most holy Father St. Benedict, namely, that the monks exercise themselves in the school of the Lord's service and ever have before their eyes the pursuit of a holy life" (Decl. 1, p. 1).

Giving this as the "primary aim" seems to point to a secondary aim, but not so. The next declaration states: "However, in accordance with that eminent discretion which our most holy Father evinces in many passages of his Rule, it is expedient to adapt our outward mode of life to the necessities and infirmities of our day, to the requirements of time and place, to the work of educating boys and young men in secondary schools as also in minor and major seminaries, to the pastoral work in parishes or in missions or for occasional assistance."

The schools and parishes of American abbeys arose because of local need, and because these were natural employments for the choir monks who were also priests. True, the first American abbeys were definitely founded as centers for missionary work among the German immigrants, and although these abbeys had a secondary end, and men entered them in order to spend their lives in the German-American parishes, these same priests knew that their motive was seeking God in the works of obedience.

When I was a young cleric at St. Meinrad's I always found the old priests who had returned to the abbey after years in the parishes good examples of this. They didn't know the theories but they indeed personified them. They knew the Holy Rule, practically by heart, and they proved the fact that the Benedictine way is essentially a mentality. These priests may have regarded obedience as the characteristic note of a Benedictine, but what was important was the *way* they viewed obedience. When the object of obedience is God, the works of obedience are totally indifferent to the monk, and they cease to be a secondary end. For obedience is carried out in simplicity and faith. The whole object is seeking God through the works of obedience.

Let us see how Cassian, who synthesized the spirituality of the Desert Fathers, saw the purpose of the monastic life. He quotes Abbot Moses as saying that the monk has an ultimate and an immediate goal. The ultimate is the kingdom of God, eternal life; "the immediate aim or goal is purity of heart, without which no one can gain that end."[2]

What is purity of heart? Cassian says that it is several things, but primarily it is charity. "Perfection is not arrived at simply by self-denial, and the giving up of all our goods, and the casting away of honors, unless there is that charity which consists in purity of heart alone."[3] Charity is that love of God which is poured into our hearts by the Holy Spirit (cf. Rom. 5:5).

The end or purpose for the monk, then, is the love of God that has been given to him, we would say *infused* love. Cassian calls this end union with God: "This then should be our main effort: and this steadfast purpose of heart we should constantly aspire after, viz., that the soul may ever cleave to God and to heavenly things."[4] He equates this union with contemplation, basing his teaching on the account of Mary and Martha. Mary has chosen "the good portion," sitting at Christ's feet, looking and listening, while Martha is out in the kitchen getting dinner. Martha's "portion can be taken away (for a bodily ministry cannot last forever with a man)," but Mary's "desire can never have an end." So too, the monk pursues the "one thing—the consideration of God alone." "You see then that the Lord makes the chief good consist in meditation, i.e., in divine contemplation."[5]

Cassian has Abbot Serenus describe the monk's end as "desiring one thing alone, thirsting for but one thing, ever bringing not only his acts but even his thoughts to bear on one thing alone, viz., that he may even now keep as an earnest [pledge] that which is said of the blessed life of the saints hereafter, that 'God may be' to him 'all in all.' "[6]

But the monk's immediate goal is not merely a pledge of that perfect contemplation of God that theology calls the Beatific Vision, but a beginning of that vision, although "in a mirror dimly" (1 Cor. 13:12), and only occasionally. Abbot Isaac, speaking of the Transfiguration, says,

Only those can look with purest eyes on his Godhead, who rise with him from low and earthly works and thoughts and go apart in the holy mountain of solitude which is free from the disturbance of all earthly thoughts and troubles, and secure from the interference of all sins, and being exalted by pure faith and the heights of virtue, God reveals the glory of his face and the image of his splendor to those who are able to look on him with pure eyes of the soul.[7]

He retired into the mountain alone to pray, thus teaching us by the example of his retirement that if we too wish to approach God with a pure and spotless affection of heart, we should also retire from all the disturbance and confusion of crowds, so that while still living in the body we may manage in some degree to adapt ourselves to some likeness of that bliss which is promised hereafter to the saints, and that 'God may be' to us 'all in all.'[8]

So we are back at purity of heart. This is not something totally negative. It does not consist merely in freedom from all desire for objects other than God and from self-will, but rather in the one desire for God alone. *Purity* must be taken in the sense of *one*: a pure substance consists of only one element—pure gold is gold alone, nothing but gold, with no alloys. When the label in a sweater proclaims that the sweater is pure wool, we know that there is no orlon, or polyester, or anything else but wool. The individual who has arrived at purity of heart has one desire, therefore he has no others. The emphasis is on the positive *one* desire, not on the absence of other desires. The monk is a person who is *all God*. There is no room for anyone or anything else. His is not a sterile purity.

The way the Benedictine wants to be at the end is the way he has to be at the beginning. The novice looks forward to his goal, the state in which God is his only desire, but he can't wait until he arrives at that state to desire God alone. He has *to start* with that desire and live and act as if the desire for God were his only desire. The process is this: if he cleaves to God he can't cleave to anything else. Worry about *attachment*, and *detachment* will take care of itself. So the way to union with God is not a system of self-improvement aimed at the perfection of the person. The novice works at acquiring the virtues and overcoming temptations to sin, but, as Abbot Moses says, he has to keep the state of union with God always in mind—"fixing our gaze then steadily on this goal, as if on a definite mark, let us direct our course as straight towards it as possible."[9]

Cassian says that "the aim of a monk, and the height of all perfection consist in the consummation of prayer."[10] Abbot Isaac, in whose conference on prayer this statement occurs, says, "The aim of every monk and the perfection of his heart tends to continual and unbroken perseverance in prayer."[11] We shall consider continual prayer in the next chapter, but it is in place to quote Abbot Isaac here to show that the end of the monk is a living and practical union with God.

A good illustration of the goal of the monk and how he must keep this goal firmly in mind as he proceeds toward it occurs in one of the sayings of the Desert Fathers:

> Abba Hilarion was asked, "How can it be right for a strenuous brother not to be offended when he seeth other monks returning to the world?" The old man said, "It is meet that he should consider the hunting dogs which follow after hares, for as one of these dogs giveth chase to the hare so soon as he seeth it (. . .), so also for the brother, who wisheth to follow after the love of Christ, is it right to fasten his gaze upon the Cross until he overtaketh him that was crucified, even though he see others who have begun to turn back."[12]

We have seen that the Benedictine is a monk in the tradition of the Desert Fathers. His fathers are St. Anthony, St. Pachomius and the multitude of Abbas whose wonderful sayings have come down to us, as well as St. Benedict. Someone has wisely called St. Benedict "the tip of the iceberg," which is to say two things. First, St. Benedict is one with the monastic tradition of the East, and second, that his Rule has best embodied this tradition for the West.

How does he put the end or goal of the monk? Does he say that the monk has only one end, or, being a practical Westerner, does he envision definite secondary ends? One would think that in view of the presence of the Teutonic barbarians in Italy, he would lay down some specific works aimed at Christianizing and civilizing these newcomers.

St. Benedict is quite definite as to the one end of his monks. There is no secondary end. A person comes to the monastery for only one purpose, and although St. Benedict expresses this goal by a variety of expressions, and although the candidate may enter with less than theocentric intentions—fear of hell, "saving his soul"—the whole life of the monastery focuses on union with God. All is organized with the attainment of that union in mind.

The novice master has to determine whether the would-be monk "truly seeks God and whether he shows eagerness for the Work of God [the Divine Office], for obedience and for trials. The novice should be clearly told all the hardships and difficulties that will lead him to God" (*RB 1980* 58, 7-8).[13]

If St. Benedict has a system or a method, it consists in the twelve steps of humility (*RB,* 7). We shall study these steps in Chapter Six, but I would like to point out here their thrust. A Benedictine begins, motivated by the fear of God, the life of seeking God in His will as that will comes to him from his abbot. If he perseveres in this life, he "will quickly arrive at that perfect love of God which casts out fear" (*RB 1980* 7, 67). His motive in climbing up the steps (or rungs) of the ladder of humility is simply his search for God. The tasks he has to do don't matter; he is seeking God in them and by means of them.

St. Benedict's road to God is obedience: "That you may return to him by the labor of obedience whom you had left by the sloth of disobedience" (*RB,* Prologue). Obedience is given not only to the abbot but to the other monks as well, "since we know that it is by this way of obedience that we go to God" (*RB 1980* 71, 2).

Going to God! That is St. Benedict's simple end for his monks. Everything in the monastery is a means and a reminder. Even the tools, pots and pans, furniture, and dishes of the monastery have a sacred character because they belong to the "house of God" (cf. *RB 1980* 31, 10 and 19).

The Benedictine way is theocentric. The monastery is a "school of the *Lord's* service" (*RB,* Prologue). Apostolates, ministries, spiritual exercises, and monastic observances: these are all so many means not ends. St. Gregory the Great called St. Benedict "the man of God," and so he was. We are reminded of the prophet of the Old Testament, who was called simply a "man of God." People work to make a name for themselves, but the only name that the monk should work for is that of "man of God," and then not to be so called but to be one.

And so through the centuries Benedictine authors have simply taken it for granted that if a person comes to a Benedictine monastery seeking entrance, one great motive has brought him or her there. The very presence of a Benedictine monastery is a concrete expression of separation from the world in order to seek God alone.

I would like to quote at length from one author—one who is our contemporary—Dom Basil Hume, former Abbot of Ampleforth in England and now Cardinal Archbishop of Westminster. In a conference to his community, which conducts a large school at the abbey and cares for a number of parishes, the then Abbot Hume said:

> The monastic life is, above all else, a search for God. It is not the acquiring of virtues, or the fostering of moral integrity; it is not carrying the Cross, it is not going flat-out at work; it is not living under obedience; it does not provide an environment for an individual to discover himself and work at his own spirituality. Any one of these would constitute a partial vision of what monasticism is. They are component parts; but they are means not ends. The end is the search for union with God. In our pastoral work our task as monks is *contemplata aliis tradere*—to hand on to others things which have been contemplated.
>
> Contemplation is not just looking at God; for most of us, now *in via*, it consists in looking *for* God, and if from time to time some "sight" of him is accorded, this will only be a glimmer granted by grace in what will always be a "cloud of unknowing." So when I use the term "contemplation" I use it in this sense: looking for God. This looking for God is done through, with, and in Christ, in unity with the Holy Spirit so that we can give, within that very life of the Trinity, all honor and glory to God, the Almighty Father. That in brief is, I think, the essence of the monastic life.[14]

The Benedictine life is contemplative and the novice has to be convinced of this, and must keep this conviction firmly in mind, or he will get lost in secondary ends and lose his vocation as a Benedictine. His work as a professed monk has to come from his union with God, and the work will drive him to union with God.

When I say *union with God* I do not mean necessarily the accomplished fact of infused contemplation, but rather the *desire* for God. This is the all-important requirement for the contemplative—the desire for God. And, like Abba Hilarion's hound, once the novice has sighted God he pursues him until he finds him, he *truly* seeks God, through all sorts of difficulties and even seeming hindrances. But nothing bothers him because he has only one end in mind.

This spirituality is simply that of the Church. There is nothing special about it, it is the way of classic Christianity. No special devotions, no systems, no methods, and no emphases. And no particular work. One monastery may have a well-frequented guest house for its work, another a school. A monastery may develop and turn out a mildly odoriferous cheese (monastic cheeses are usually mildly odoriferous), or a distillation that is marked as a "tonic." But through the stacks of cheeses, bubbling liqueurs, and noisome boys, the monk is quietly pursuing God. I say *quietly* because this pursuit is not a frenzied chase, overturning cheeses, etc., but a peaceful, dogged, relentless one that is more like Hercule Poirot using his "little grey cells" to achieve his end.

NOTES

[1]D. Cuthbertus Butler, *Sancti Benedicti Regula Monasteriorum* (Freiburg: Herder and Co., 1935), p. 159. Author's translation.

[2]John Cassian, *Conferences,* in Rev. Edgar C. S. Gibson, tr., *Nicene and Post-Nicene Fathers* (Grand Rapids, MI: William B. Eerdmans Publishing Co, 1964), Vol. XI, p. 296, First Conference of Abbot Moses, ch. 4.

[3]*Ibid.,* p. 297, ch. 6.

[4]*Ibid.,* p. 298, ch. 8.

[5]*Ibid.*

[6]*Ibid.,* p. 365, First Conference of Abbot Serenus, ch. 6.

[7]*Ibid.,* p. 403, Second Conference of Abbot Isaac, ch. 6.

[8]*Ibid.*

[9]*Ibid.,* p. 296, First Conference of Abbot Moses, ch. 4.

[10]*Ibid.,* p. 390, First Conference of Abbot Isaac, ch. 7.

[11]*Ibid.,* p. 387, *ibid.,* ch. 2.

[12]E. A. Wallis Budge, *The Paradise of the Holy Fathers* (London: Chatto & Windus, 1907), Vol. II, p. 199. Cf. Walter Hilton, *The Scale of Perfection* (Westminster, MD: The Newman Press, 1953), pp. 59-60. Hilton borrows Abba Hilarion's example of the hunting dog who has once sighted the hare, and draws appropriate conclusions.

[13]*RB 1980* means the translation in the book of that name, edited by Timothy Fry, OSB (Collegeville, MN: The Liturgical Press, 1980). *RB* means another translation, often the author's.

[14]Basil Hume, OSB, *Searching for God* (Wilton, CT: Morehouse-Barlow Co. Inc., 1978), pp. 100-101. Cf. also Jean Leclercq, *The Love of Learning and the Desire for God* (New York: The Fordham University Press, 1962), pp. 27-28.

II
Continual Prayer

WE HAVE SEEN, IN CHAPTER I, Abbot Moses express the end of the monk as union with God—"that the soul may ever cleave to God and to heavenly things"—and clarify this cleaving as divine contemplation.[1] We have also seen Abbot Isaac, showing the way to this contemplation, stating that, "The aim of every monk and the perfection of his heart tends to continual and unbroken perseverance in prayer."[2] Union with God and continual prayer are really one and the same thing. This fact is obvious. It is easier to see that seeking God—the process whereby one arrives at union—means, in practice, continual prayer.

The Benedictine wants to go to God simply and directly, and for him this is the best way. So whether he knows it or not—and often he isn't aware of it—his life becomes a continual prayer. I say "becomes" because the seeking God and the going to God take work, and the monk may have to work at these activities all his life. Actually he is always in the process of becoming a monk. The continual prayer is not the hard part of a monk's life, but rather keeping in mind and heart the one end. Once he seeks God, and seeking, finds him, prayer is easy because it comes from the heart. His life will become a continual prayer as he becomes a monk.

Cassian tells monks and would-be monks in his *Institutes* that the wandering thoughts of the mind should be "restrained by continual recollection of God. And the slippery wanderings of our heart should be brought back again to the contemplation of God as often as our crafty enemy, in his endeavor to lead away the mind a captive from this consideration, creeps into the innermost recesses of the heart."[3]

The idea of continual prayer was something that the first monks took for granted because St. Paul had said, "Pray constantly" (1 Thess. 5:17). And if St. Paul had said it, then it was something that Christians did, therefore that monks did.

Abbot Isaac gives a particular reason for this injunction. He speaks about the need to be free from distractions during the monk's periods of prayer, what we know today as the Divine Office, and those times we set aside for personal prayer.

> For whatever our mind has been thinking of before the hour of prayer, is sure to occur to us while we are praying through the activity of the memory. Wherefore what we want to find ourselves like while we are praying, that we ought to prepare ourselves to be before the time for prayer. And therefore if we do not want anything to haunt us while we are praying, we should be careful before our prayer, to exclude it from the shrine of our heart, that we may thus fulfill the Apostle's injunction: 'Pray without ceasing' (1 Thess. 5:17); and 'in every place lifting up holy hands without wrath or disputing' (1 Tm. 2:8).[4]

Cassian's mentors, the Desert Fathers, take continual prayer as one of the things a monk necessarily does. An anonymous abba said: "The soul hath need of the four following virtues at all seasons: A man must pray without ceasing and . . . pour himself out before God continually, and he should declare his own defects in his heart, and he should judge no man, and his own mind should be tranquil."[5]

Abba Epiphanius said: "Know thyself, and thou shalt never fall. Give thy soul work, that is to say, constant prayer, and love of God, before another can give it evil and filthy thoughts; and pray ye that the spirit of error may be remote from you."[6]

Abba Sisoes was one of the early "greats" of the Egyptian desert. After spending most of his long life as a hermit—seventy-two years alone on St. Anthony's mountain—he was brought to a monastery where the monks could take care of him in his extreme old age. There he did not enjoy the solitude he had been used to because the monks came into his room every day for, as they would put it, "a word to live by." He wasn't accustomed to company and certainly not a crowd. We can sympathize with the poor old man, famous but now feeble and only wanting to be able to live in silence and to die in peace.

One day another great old man, Abba Ammon, came to visit him, and he chided Sisoes for being unhappy in his new home because he was being well taken care of. Sisoes replied that, although he could no longer perform the "labors of the body," he was today "better able to perform the labors of the mind" because of a long life spent in recollection, but the constant stream of visitors to his cell was a great distraction and he missed what he called his "freedom of the thoughts."

He gives, in his complaint, a beautiful description of the basic work of monks:

> ...the clear shining of the mind, which a monk acquireth by a life of contemplation in silence, and the constant intercourse with God, and the prayer which is without ceasing, and the remembrance of Christ, and the constant gazing upon him, and the exultation of the soul in him, and the favor of his love, and the affection for his commandments, and the desire for his good things, and the meditation upon his glory, and the thought about his excellence and his majesty, and the admiration of his humility.[7]

We note in these passages that the Desert Fathers call continual prayer work for the mind and heart. This is so because their daily manual work was one that required no thinking, or at least only an occasional thought or two whenever they hit a snag—weaving baskets and making ropes out of palm leaves. Such an occupation was clearly one for the body, an automatic process that they could do in their sleep (and, knowing their penchant for vigils, probably did). You are thinking of the contemporary Benedictine and all of the work in a modern monastery. There are times when doing nothing but turning a pile of soggy palm fronds into baskets looks pretty good, and one longs for Abba Sisoes' "labors of the mind." It would all be so simple and easy!

Yet Cardinal Hume, when abbot of a very active abbey, said to his novices: "A monastic life is a poor one if prayer does not have the primacy in the mind of the monk. In whatever circumstances a monk finds himself; whatever the calls of schoolwork or his parish (these are necessary, even, at times, imperative), if these demands diminish the primacy in his life of prayer, to that extent his vocation is defective. There can be no compromise here."[8]

So how does the modern Benedictine do it? We shall pursue the answer to that question in the course of this chapter. But now, after airing objections, let us return to the Desert Fathers.

A brother asked an old man, "What limit ought there be to prayer?"

And the old abba replied: "No measure hath been laid down to prayer; because He said, 'Pray ye at all times and continually,' He did not lay down any measure to prayer. For if the monk only really prayeth when he standeth up in prayer, he who is thus doth not pray with the heart but with the mouth only."[9]

"Standing up in prayer" was apparently a spiritual exercise—psalmody at fixed hours of the day and night, or a definite period of personal prayer. What the old man is saying to us today is that liturgy without continual prayer is a formal exercise, "with the mouth only." Prayer is not only for stated times but for always.

What does St. Benedict have to say about continual prayer? He does not prescribe it in these or similar words, but he actually does demand it because of his approach to the monastic life. Here is where understanding the Benedictine way is important.

Because St. Benedict sees the objective of the monk as the pursuit of God, that uppermost thought forms the basis for his continual prayer. I would like to save his teaching on this for the second part of this chapter where we consider the practical aspect of the subject, the "how to" about praying continually. St. Benedict is always practical, which is the reason why I think he never says "continual prayer" as such. He knows that if he did, some over-zealous monks might be needing psychiatric help.

One of St. Benedict's most famous sons is Father Augustine Baker (1575-1641), whose short treatises were gathered, after his death, into a book entitled *Holy Wisdom* (or *Sancta Sophia*). Father Baker was a great proponent of the fact that Benedictines are to be contemplatives. Building on Christ's injunction to his disciples to pray always (Lk. 18:1), and St. Paul's to the Thessalonians to "pray constantly" (1 Thess. 5:17), Father Baker insists that not only Benedictines, but all Christians have the duty of continual prayer.[10] He has this to say to Benedictines: "This is the perfection of prayer to which our holy Rule obliges us to aspire, namely, besides the set exercises either of vocal or internal prayer, to preserve our souls in an uninterrupted attention to God and tendance in spirit to him, so as that whatsoever actions we do, they should be with a most fervent and perseverant prayer."[11] Father

Baker is very practical; *Holy Wisdom* has been for centuries the manual of the English Benedictine Congregation.

Thus, all of our great authors understand that a Benedictine practices continual prayer, because his vocation is to live conscious of God. All of our saints have so lived, and became saints because they did. We have no other way.

One hears and reads today the expression "prayer life," which, as people use it, means the praying they do in their daily life. It implies a dichotomy—now I pray, now I work, now I recreate, etc. Not so for the Benedictine. He has no "prayer life" in this sense but a life of prayer. Abbot Columba Marmion, whose *Christ the Ideal of the Monk* has become a classic for Benedictines, favors this latter expression. He has some beautiful pages on this subject to which I can only refer you. But I would like to extract several sentences that give us an idea of his thought: "Happy that soul that lives in inward silence, the fruit of a calm imagination, of the rejection of vain solicitude and heedless haste, of the quelling of the passions, of progress in solid virtue, of the concentration of the faculties upon the constant seeking after the Only Good!... Let us then live in recollection and try to remain closely united to our Lord."[12]

*   *   *

We come now to that promised section about how we are to pray always. Again, we must turn first to our ancestors, the Desert Fathers, to see what they did and taught.

Their basic idea, or method, of continual prayer was living conscious of God's presence. "Always have God before your eyes," said St. Anthony, the father of monks.[13] And Abba Macarius said that a monk ought "to be constantly before God."[14] "Abba Theona used to say, 'Because we put ourselves out of the sight of God we are led captive by the passions of the body.' "[15]

We cannot "put ourselves out of the sight of God," but we can forget his presence, and that's when we get into trouble. Therefore we must always realize that we are living in God's sight. He is looking at us, and we are looking at him. This need not always be a conscious "looking," which would be impossible, but what is possible is comparable to what happens in ordinary daily life. When two friends are together, or a husband and wife, each may be occupied with his own pursuits, but each is also basically aware that the other is present. When one speaks, the other is not startled because, in spite of his preoccupation with what he is doing, he knew the other was there all along.

It is good to use our imagination in realizing God's presence. An anonymous old abba said that the prophets had visions of God under various appearances and added wisely, "And what is the better for a man, to depict God in his mind in this manner, or to bow himself down to many abominable thoughts?"[16] In other words, in the context of continual prayer, we should fight images with images. I have already quoted Abba Sisoes in this chapter as to the Christocentric nature of his continual prayer—"the remembrance of Christ, and the constant gazing upon him." Christ is "the image of the invisible God" and it helps to have a mental picture of him, or one of his mysteries, present before us (or within us). We don't stop with his humanity, of course, because he is also God, but the way to his divinity is through his human nature.

How did the Desert Fathers pray as they did their manual work? Abba Lucius told some visitors his method: "While doing my manual work, I pray without interruption. I sit down with God, soaking my reeds and plaiting my ropes, and I say, 'God, have mercy on me; according to your great goodness and according to the multitude of your mercies, save me from my sins.' "[17]

This short prayer reminds us of the Jesus Prayer. I believe that we can find the origin of this prayer in Abba Ammon's advice to a monk. Abba Ammon was a disciple of St. Anthony, which fact places him among the pioneer Desert Fathers. He said: "Sit in thy cell, and eat a very little food every day, and let there be in thine heart always the words of the publican, 'God be merciful to me a sinner,' and thus thou shall be able to live" (cf. Lk. 18:13).[18]

After reading the Desert Fathers I made this definition: A monk is one who guards his thoughts, doesn't get angry, doesn't judge others, and prays continually. These four points run through the sayings of the Fathers as constants. Of course, guarding one's thoughts would take care of the rest. Guarding one's thoughts complements continual prayer, safeguards it, and leads to it. It's a check on oneself, a reminder that one's mind is wandering needlessly. And real prayer certainly forces a discipline on the mind that makes for control. Guarding our thoughts can even be considered a method of continual prayer if we return our wandering mind back to the thought of God. The exercise has to be done, not for self-improvement, but for prayer.

But the best method of continual prayer after all is the simple seeking of God alone. An old man said, "The palm tree has a single heart, which is white, containing all that is good. One meets the same thing amongst the righteous: their heart is simple, seeing only God; it is white, having the illumination which proceeds from faith; and all the work of the righteous is in their hearts."[19] The heart is a person's deepest desire, and the Benedictine's deepest desire must be for God. His heart, then, is single and simple. He has one intention in all that he does and omits. Hence the thought of God is uppermost in his mind, and from this continual dominant thought proceeds his prayer without ceasing. The process is: desire, intention, attention, prayer.

I can see difficulties rising in your minds, and even the desert monks questioned this ideal of continual prayer. One of them asked: "But suppose I be talking to someone, how is it possible for me to fulfill the command, 'Be ye praying continually'?" An old abba answered thus: "Now concerning this the Apostle spake, 'In all your prayers, and in all your supplications, pray ye at all times in the spirit; and when it would be unseemly for thee to pray, because thou art speaking with another man, pray thou through supplication.' "[20] The Apostle didn't quite say all that—the old man made an application of Ephesians 6:18—but his application is a valid one and it certainly answers the question.

"Supplication" here means the prayer of petition (although Cassian sees it as asking God's pardon for our sins). What the old abba is saying is that when the monk is with others and has to talk, either out of charity or necessity, he can still pray by praying silently for them. I think that we do this more often than we realize. Conversation, like soap operas, is usually about trouble, the other person's trouble. The monk is a good listener. And during the other person's recital the monk, while making compassionate sounds, is also lifting mind and heart to pray for him.

A monk's work, which today is often more complex than plaiting baskets, can lead him to prayer, frequent prayer which in effect places him in a state of prayer. Work like this can be a practical means to the contemplative life for many who would sink into boredom floating about in a cloister garth.

To restate the problem, Cassian's companion, Germanus, put a valid objection to Abbot Moses:

> "Who then, while he is burdened with our frail flesh, can be always so intent on this contemplation, as never to think about the arrival of a brother, or visiting the sick, or manual labor, or at least about showing kindness to strangers and visitors? And lastly, who is not interrupted by providing for the body, and looking after it? Or how and in what way can the mind cling to the invisible and incomprehensible God? This we should like to learn."
>
> Moses replied: "To cling to God continually and, as you say, inseparably, to hold fast to meditation on him, is impossible for a man while still in this weak flesh of ours. But we ought to be aware on what we should have the purpose of our mind fixed, and to what goal we should ever recall the gaze of our soul; and when the mind can secure this it may rejoice, and grieve and sigh when it is withdrawn from this, and as often as it discovers itself to have fallen away from gazing on him, it should admit that it has lapsed from the highest good, considering that even a momentary departure from gazing on Christ is fornication. And when our gaze has wandered ever so little from him, let us turn the eyes of the soul back to him, and recall our mental gaze as in a perfectly straight direction."[21]

Notice the words "purpose" and "goal" in the above passage. Then note the words "gaze" and "gazing." A concentrated and intent prayer is not always possible, not only because of the monk's daily duties, but also because of the "weak flesh." But what *is* possible is the keeping of the monk's one end uppermost in his mind, in pursuing union with God in and through all that he does. Monks and nuns want union with God, hence they are ever looking for him or at him. This "gazing on Christ" comes naturally to the person who does all his activities because Christ wills them.

St. Benedict's methods of continual prayer are very simple and basic—nothing more than those of the Desert Fathers. Particular "acts" are not to be said by all when the clock strikes; beads are not handed out. Benedictines are free to pray as they want, so long as they remember that they are monks and nuns, and therefore pray as monks and nuns. The Benedictine has great freedom within the framework of the monastic life.

One way the individual will pray continually is by being always conscious of God's presence. St. Benedict's "ascetical method" is mounting the twelve rungs of the ladder of humility (*RB*, chapter 7). These twelve rungs (degrees, steps) he took from the Rule of the Master, but he made them his own because they apparently work, and they fit into his overall plan. (In Chapter Six, "The Benedictine Way," we shall study St. Benedict's twelve steps of humility. There we shall look further into the topic of realizing God's presence as St. Benedict presents it in his treatment of the first step.) "The first step of humility, then, is that a man keeps the fear of God always before his eyes and never forgets it."[22] "Let him recall that he is always seen by God in heaven, that his actions everywhere are in God's sight and are reported by angels at every hour."[23] This awareness is the basis for Benedictine continual prayer. The monk begins with this. Whether he wants to think of God as in heaven, before him, or within him, it doesn't matter. What matters is that he acquire the habit of continual awareness of God's presence.

I know this smacks of "God is watching me, look out!" But what the first step of humility attempts to achieve is twofold: that the person begin to realize God's presence, and that he should understand the difference between God and himself. The more one grasps the fact that God is God and I am only his creature, the more apt one is to remember the continual presence of this almighty, all-necessary, all-demanding Being. And, of course, the more one realizes the difference between God and self the more one is going to obey God. This is St. Benedict's "fear of God"—not a terrorized cringing but a "getting the true picture" and acting accordingly.

The chapter in the Rule on the proper dispositions a monk should have when praying the Divine Office opens with these words: "We believe that the divine presence is everywhere and that in every place the eyes of the Lord are watching the good and the wicked. But beyond the least doubt we should believe this to be especially true when we celebrate the Divine Office."[24]

Here is St. Benedict's fundamental point, the foundation of his spirituality, in short, his method. Granted the facts that God exists and that I exist, and that I am a human being with intellect and free will, I must realize that God is present to me and I to him. It's a case of mutual *dasein*. My whole life as a monk is growing in the realization and experience of God present to me. To even think of continual prayer as such is to dichotomize. My life with God becomes a simple, undivided, single experience which naturally includes prayer.

Note in this passage the opening words, "We believe." Realization of God's presence depends on faith, and faith is something supernatural and has to be prayed for. We do not see God with our eyes; he is not perceptible by the senses. So to live always aware of God's presence we have to ask him for faith, to see him with the eyes of faith, and to renew our consciousness of his presence often, and to bring ourselves back from other absorbing thoughts.

In the beginning of one's monastic life the novice should really work at acquiring the habit of this continual awareness of God. And even for us who have been in the monastery for years, we find it necessary to work at it. A person gets lazy, or too professional, or self-satisfied, or trapped in a rut of his own making. We, too, must say very often, "My God, you are here, within me and without. I live before your eyes."

St. Benedict says in the beginning of the Prologue to the Rule, "First of all, every time you begin a good work, you must pray to him most earnestly to bring it to perfection."[25] He wisely knows the need to renew one's faith in God's presence, with all that that presence includes. Benedictines spend so much of their day seeking God in his will. They have to stop and recognize God's will, his presence in that will, and know for a certainty that it is really God who is going "to bring it to perfection." The Latin for "most earnestly" is *instantissima* which can be translated as *vehemently*. In either case the idea is that this prayer must be a serious attempt to "get through to" God, and not be a perfunctory and dutiful token, as grace before meals can so often be.

For the purpose of renewing one's awareness of God's presence, St.

Benedict says in his list of tools: "devote yourself often to prayer."[26] Actually the Latin conveys the idea that the monk should prostrate himself often in prayer. Praying in a prostrate position was common in his time and during the Middle Ages—nothing like using the whole person to remind one of God's presence. It would be a little awkward to prostrate from time to time during the tasks modern monks and nuns have to do, but all can at least mentally interrupt their work to pray often. And until God gives us an infused continual awareness of him, it becomes absolutely necessary to do this. *In order to pray continually we have to pray often.* We can see this as one of St. Benedict's methods. You may object that your work demands all your attention, but if you have prayed before you began, that God would "bring it to perfection," you ought to remind yourself, during it, that it is *God* who is principally at work.

To prostrate oneself often in prayer demands that the Benedictine *interrupt* his work often and concentrate on God. The work is going to suffer? Better the work than the person! This interruption reminds us that we have only one end, and that we seek *God*, and find him, in and through our work. Thus work done by Benedictines should be different from that done by others.

Two more of St. Benedict's tools are these: "To keep guard at all times over the actions of one's life. To know for certain that God sees one in every place."[27] Here we have a re-wording of the Desert Fathers' principle, that the monk must guard his thoughts, with the reason given in the first step of humility—God is present, God knows! We can see these two as complementing each other with regard to continual prayer: we will always be aware of God's presence if we keep guard over our thoughts at all times, bringing our wandering mind and will back to God. It's the desert method of constant custody.

Another desert method that St. Benedict adopts is memorizing the psalms and other parts of the Bible. During the winter season, "from the first of November until Easter," there would be quite an interval between the end of Vigils and the beginning of Lauds at daybreak. This interval was not to be spent in bed. "In the time remaining after Vigils, those who need to learn some of the psalter or readings should study them."[28] He means by this that the monks should learn by heart the psalms and the biblical readings and selections from the Fathers of the Church that occur in the Divine Office.

Of course, the immediate reason for this activity was ease in singing the psalms and lessons in the dark oratory, lit only by candles and equipped with a minimum of books. For this reason the monks had to memorize their Office. But a secondary reason was the ability to pray the psalms and repeat parts of the Bible aloud during their work and at other times.

Today lack of books and poor lighting are not the problem. Bibles and psalters we have, and in a variety of translations, and sometimes the contemporary monk or nun has all of them. Because we don't *have* to memorize, we don't memorize. We see no reason for doing so. Yet biblical passages known by heart provide a means for prayer outside of the Divine Office, at least some of the time. We are free in this regard; nevertheless memorized psalms are a Benedictine means to continual prayer. Many psalms become favorites of ours. Why not memorize these? The biographer of St. Wulstan, an Anglo-Saxon monk of the eleventh century, says of him, "Semper in ore psalmus," "Always a psalm in his mouth."

The hours that St. Benedict wants the monks to spend in *lectio divina,* sacred reading, are hours devoted in part to memorizing, especially the Bible.[29] Since the Bible is regarded as the word of God, the monk is always able to listen to God speaking to him in the passages that he has learned by heart and repeats to himself both during the hours of reading and other times of the day. He need never plead that he is at a loss as to what to pray about. His mind is well-stocked with biblical texts. All he has to do is listen, and make his response.

To insure that his monks learned the spirituality of the desert, St. Benedict specified that Cassian's *Conferences* or the *Lives of the Fathers* be read aloud before Compline. The latter would include lives of some of the great abbas of the desert. He allows for other works to be read instead, but these two books he specifies. Thus the monks would be aware of the continual prayer of their monastic ancestors, and of their methods.[30] Cassian's *Conferences* and *Institutes* and the *Lives* are recommended for private reading, coming, in St. Benedict's listing, after the Bible and the Fathers, in the final chapter of the Rule.[31]

St. Benedict's insistence on silence is proverbial. Some paintings and statues portray him with finger on lips.[32] While silence certainly eliminates the opportunity for sins of the tongue, it equally provides an atmosphere in which the Benedictine can pray always. In fact, the very restraint that he has to place on his tongue is a reminder to pray. And the freedom from distraction and the noise which many today can't seem to live without makes one realize that silence is the language of love, and certainly the means of communicating in the Trinity.

＊　　　＊　　　＊

In summary, then, a Benedictine has come to the monastery for *union* with God, a union of the loving God with his loving self. He knows from his knowledge of love that when two people truly love each other they obey each other because love is the union of wills—willing each other's good. And he knows that loving God is the same thing: willing what God wills. The way to authentic union with God is the way of obedience, any other way is false. He comes to realize the word of Christ, "You are my friends if you do what I command you" (Jn. 15:14). He begins as a servant, searching for God, and he ends up as a friend, finding God in his will. All along he has had only one desire, and no matter what works God has willed him to do, this desire has been uppermost and constant. He has actually been living in an atmosphere of prayer, because prayer is basically the desire for God.

To seek God is to find him, so the Benedictine who sincerely and unrelentingly seeks God alone is living with him. His intention is his method of continual prayer.

St. Benedict's specific instructions serve as aids to insure and intensify this intention. Guarding the thoughts—what is this other than guarding one's intention? Praying frequently is a reminder in a distracting day to pray always. And praying "vehemently" at the beginning of an activity is simply a means to keep attentive to God throughout it.

Memorized biblical passages repeated to oneself during the day are springboards to prayer as well as means of listening to God. A person may not find this practice practical during his work, but it is ideal for "oases" times. Praying before an activity and the need of oases times make him realize that he has to have longer periods of personal prayer, apart from the Divine Office and Mass. His continual prayer is really going to depend ultimately on these periods and on his prayer during them.

Within St. Benedict's framework the Benedictine has great liberty. He may like the Jesus Prayer or the Rosary as a means of frequently devoting himself to prayer (*RB* 4, 56); he may simply prefer an awareness of God's presence. This latter may not always be so acute, but he *is aware*. The Benedictine Rule in this matter is *whatever works*. Our Lord said it first: results are the proof of authenticity. And the first result has to be peace—Benedictine *pax*—the peace that the monk has, particularly in the more exacting duties and problems in his day.

If we really live the life of the Rule we will come to continual prayer. The thing is to live the life and not be anxious. This is St. Benedict's way. For the anxious there is Abbot Chapman's dictum, *Solvitur ambulando*: problems solve themselves as we go along.

The best conclusion for this chapter, and the secret of continual prayer, is the word of the psalmist, "With my whole heart I seek thee!" (Ps. 119:10).

NOTES

[1] Cassian, *Conferences*, in Rev. Edgar C. S. Gibson, tr., *Nicene and Post-Nicene Fathers* (Grand Rapids: Wm. B. Eerdmans Publishing Co., 1964), Vol. XI, p. 298.

[2] *Ibid.*, p. 387.

[3] *Ibid.*, p. 237, *Institutes*, Bk. V, ch. 10.

[4] *Ibid.*, p. 388, First Conference of Abbot Isaac, ch. 3.

[5] E. A. Wallis Budge, *The Paradise of the Holy Fathers* (London: Chatto and Windus, 1907), Vol. II, pp. 277-278.

[6] *Ibid.*, p. 27.

[7]*Ibid.*, pp. 320-321. Sister Benedicta Ward, S.L.G., gives a very shortened version of this in her *The Desert Christian* (New York: Macmillan Publishing Co., Inc., 1980), pp. 217-218.

[8]Cardinal George Basil Hume, O.S.B., *Searching for God* (Wilton, CT: Morehouse-Barlow Co., Inc., 1978), pp. 55-56.

[9]Budge, *op. cit.*, p. 275. Cf. p. 274, no. 594.

[10]Cf. Augustine Baker, *Holy Wisdom* (Wheathampstead, Hertfordshire: Anthony Clarke Books, 1972), pp. 314-317.

[11]*Ibid.*, p. 317.

[12]Dom Columba Marmion, O.S.B., *Christ The Ideal of the Monk* (St. Louis: B. Herder Book Co., 1926), p. 363. Cf. pp. 361-371.

[13]Ward, *The Desert Christian*, p. 2.

[14]Budge, *op. cit.*, II, p. 192.

[15]*Ibid.*, p. 253.

[16]*Ibid.*, p. 273.

[17]Ward, *op. cit.*, p. 121.

[18]Budge, *op. cit.*, II, p. 105. (Cf. Ward, *op. cit.*, p. 26.)

[19]Sister Benedicta Ward, *The Wisdom of the Desert Fathers* (Oxford: SLG Press, 1975), pp. 62-63. Cf. Budge, *op. cit.*, II, p. 195.

[20]Budge, *op. cit.*, II, pp. 274-275.

[21]Cassian's *Conferences*, p. 300, First Conference of Abbot Moses, chs. 12-13.

[22]Timothy Fry, O.S.B., ed., *RB 1980* (Collegeville, MN: The Liturgical Press, 1980), 7, 10, p. 193. Psalm 36:2 is quoted.

[23]*Ibid.*, 7, 13, p. 195. The whole first step should be read.

[24]*Ibid.*, 19, 1-2, pp. 215-216.

[25]*Ibid.*, Prologue 4, p. 159.

[26]*Ibid.*, 4, 56, p. 185.

[27]*Rule of St. Benedict* 4, 48-49.

[28]*RB 1980* 8, 3.

[29]*Ibid.*, ch. 48.

[30]*Ibid.*, ch. 42.

[31]*Ibid.*, ch. 73.

[32]*Ibid.*, chs. 6; 7, 65-68; 38, 5-9; 42, 1 and 8-11; 52, 2-5; 53, 23-24.

III
Periods of Prayer

PRAYER IS THE ESSENCE of the Benedictine life. Because monks and nuns have one purpose—to seek God alone—they seek God continually in prayer, and, finding him, enjoy living with him. Therefore they want times when they can devote themselves uninterruptedly to more concentrated prayer, spaces in the day—which is a busy one—when they can dismiss the crowd and, with Christ, go up into the hills to pray. Periods of prayer will nourish continual prayer and give meaning to the Divine Office and the Eucharist.

What does St. Benedict say about these periods of prayer? Does he prescribe, as later Rules and Constitutions will, a definite time and length for meditation and spiritual reading? St. Benedict does not know this distinction between meditation and spiritual reading. It will come later with the "invention" of a methodical exercise known henceforth in Catholic spirituality as meditation, methodical to the point, in most instances, of a highly structured technique. St. Benedict knows only one "exercise," which he calls *lectio divina,* and about its time and length he is quite clear.

Apart from this *lectio* he writes about times for prayer that are personal and spontaneous. In Chapter 52, on the oratory of the monastery, he says, "After the Work of God, all should leave in complete silence and with reverence for God, so that a brother who may wish to pray alone will not be disturbed by the insensitivity of another. Moreover, if at other times someone chooses to pray privately, he may simply go in and pray, not in a loud voice, but with tears and heartfelt devotion" (*RB 1980* 52, 2-4).

Monks can pray privately anyplace, and should, but St. Benedict is writing of private prayer in the oratory which, because it is a public place, can attract those whose manner of praying is distracting to others. What matters here is that monks *do* pray privately, and that they should. They take time to do so, even for long periods.

We can see why this is so from what St. Benedict says personal prayer should be. "Tears and heartfelt devotion" ought to give us some idea. And what he says about personal prayer in Chapter 20 goes deeper: "We must know that God regards our purity of heart and tears of compunction, not our many words. Prayer should therefore be short and pure, unless perhaps it is prolonged under the inspiration of divine grace" (*RB 1980* 20, 3-4).

The Benedictine who is working at union with God, who becomes aware of God as his only Good, and the gap his sins have created between himself and God, is going to run to these times when he can pour out his heart to God without fear of distraction and pressure of immediate duty. These times may be brief, but they should be intense. And God's grace can and will prolong them, so that he forgets time.

They are like coffee breaks, or "the pause that refreshes," and the individual will want and need these times. They are not perfunctory visits to the Blessed Sacrament, nor limited to one or two a day. They are a matter of desire, of wanting God alone. St. Benedict doesn't legislate for these times, and neither should he. What he does legislate for are definite periods of prayer in the monastic timetable. These periods, while not spontaneous, exist so that the monk can pray spontaneously.

St. Benedict begins Chapter 48, "The Daily Manual Labor," with these words: "Idleness is the enemy of the soul. Therefore, the brother should have specified periods for manual labor as well as for prayerful reading" (*RB 1980* 48, 1). "Prayerful reading" translates *lectio divina,* literally *divine reading. Divine* tells us what the Benedictine should read; if he reads this material the way a monk should, such activity will result in personal prayer.

In this chapter, St. Benedict states what times the community should devote to *lectio divina.* Because he wants his monks to live by the sun, these times will differ in summer and winter. But there will always be a minimum of two hours of *lectio* in summer, when the longer day allows for more manual work, and in winter about two to three hours during the morning and another hour in the afternoon.

In Lent the monks will read from five o'clock in the morning until nine with a break at sunrise for Prime. On Sunday all but the most necessary manual work ceases, so the monks will have all the time that they would normally devote to work during the week to read. That could add up to some ten hours!

Reading is not busy-work, as the opening sentence of Chapter 48 would seem to imply. *Lectio divina* is a necessity for the monastic, along with the liturgy, private prayer, and work. St. Benedict makes it an essential part of the day and underlines its importance by the amount of time he wants devoted to it. In fact, it is the place and space that *lectio divina* enjoys in the monastic horarium that indicates the fact that Benedictines are to be contemplatives in the strict sense. Of course, this insistence on *lectio* follows from the fact that Benedictines live in the Desert tradition. St. Benedict is simply continuing the monastic tradition.

Why is *lectio divina* a preparation for infused contemplation? The term tells us that in this kind of reading the Benedictine is reading the words of God—*divine* reading. Actually he listens to God speaking, and he makes his response. It is a time for the person to seek God directly and to find him, for God to reveal himself and his plan. *Lectio divina* means One-to-one, Person-to-person.

The material read during this *lectio* is God's revelation, that is, the Bible, the Fathers of the Church, and, I might add, those classic works that give us authentic insights into God's word. The Bible, as we have seen in the last chapter, was *the* book of the Desert Fathers, who learned much, and in some cases all of it, by heart. God's revelation comes to us in two forms: the Bible and Tradition.[1] The writings of the Church Fathers provide an important source of Tradition.

Our monastic ancestors said that in the Bible God speaks to us, and in prayer we speak to God. In the Bible God reveals his plan for mankind, his purpose. God shows himself always in relation to us; we look in the Bible in vain for a theological tract on God—One and Three. What the transcendent, hidden God tells us about himself is always functional, practical. And what he tells us about ourselves is never theoretical but practical—what we are, and how we should act toward God and others. *Pragmatic* would be a good description of God's revelation in the Bible.

God reveals his plan gradually, adapting himself to human beings as he finds them. But the plan is all there in the Genesis account of man's creation: a handful of earth enlivened by God's breath, a person, an image of his Creator. God's plan is that this person is to live by his breath-Spirit! But this person refused to accept the Lordship of God, refused the life of a child of God, the Spirit. God's ultimate plan was to restore this life and bestow the status of an adopted child of his through his own Son-become-man. This is what God is telling us in the Bible. That God is actually three Persons is revealed as God unfolds his purpose for mankind.

In the Bible God is speaking to each one of us personally. True, he spoke to Israel, and to the Church, but we are the persons in the Church, and we have to listen to him as if we were *there*, present in the original group to whom he spoke. He does not mean one thing for you and another for me. No, he has one meaning for everyone in the whole group, but how many in the group are attentive to him? We listen to him *now*, carefully and openly. *Now* we understand what he is saying because now we are listening. And he will let us understand the depths of what he is saying. "To him who has will more be given."

What God said to Abraham then he is saying to me now. What he did for Israel then, his saving acts during the Exodus, he does and will do for the Church, for me. So when I open my Bible I begin a conversation with God. He speaks, he always speaks, I listen, and speak to him. It should be evident that the hours devoted to *lectio divina* are hours devoted to union with God and to personal prayer.

This has to be the case because St. Benedict, in consonance with monastic tradition, presumes that the Bible is the first and principal reading material of his monks. It could be for many their only reading material, when we realize that most of the Church Fathers' writings were simply commentaries on the books of the Bible. Too, a monk would stay with the Bible and its commentaries until he had learned it in its essentials by heart, or at least had made its contents part of himself. This could take up his whole life![2]

The writings of the Fathers of the Church will also provide material for *lectio*. These giants of the first centuries of the Church stand out as witnesses to what the Church was teaching in those times, therefore as witnesses to the faith of the Church. St. Benedict calls them "catholic

Fathers," because they represent what was believed by all, everywhere. They have written down what the Church, under the guidance of the Holy Spirit, was doing with the teaching of Christ. And their Spirit-inspired insights developed this teaching.

The Fathers did not merely repeat the Bible, they related its great themes and drew conclusions. They were indeed creative theologians. As I have said above, they all left commentaries on the Bible, whether as such, or in their treatises. The early Benedictine monks naturally turned to these as helps to understand the Bible.

Did the early monks have any procedure for *lectio divina*, something comparable to a method? Yes, and fortunately we are rather well-informed about it. Some of this procedure, the heart of it, we know already—God speaking to the monk and the monk speaking to God. But there was a definite procedure and we must look at this and see what we can learn from this for our own *lectio divina*.

First of all, the early monks read aloud, and not just their *lectio*, but everything. Everybody in ancient times, and even into the Middle Ages, read aloud, not loudly, of course, but to themselves. (The fabled Silence signs in modern libraries probably replaced those in the libraries of antiquity that read Mumble.) St. Augustine was amazed that his mentor, St. Ambrose, read silently.

Dom Jean Leclercq has called our attention to this fact in his *The Love of Learning and the Desire for God*. He writes:

> In the Middle Ages, as in antiquity, they read usually, not as today principally with the eyes, but with the lips, pronouncing what they saw, and with the ears, listening to the words pronounced, hearing what is called "the voices of the pages." It is a real acoustical reading; *legere* means at the same time *audire*; one understands only what one hears, as we still say: "entendre le latin," which means to "comprehend" it.[3]

Notice here Dom Leclercq's strong statement that these people read principally with their lips and ears!

St. Benedict permits a siesta during spring and summer, but he allows for non-nappers in the common dormitory who might want to read: "If perhaps one should wish to read alone, let him so read as not to disturb anyone else" (*RB*, ch. 48). Thus the buzz of voices would not keep the others awake.

Another practice that the monks had when they read—they memorized. In the last chapter we saw that the monks memorized a good part of the Divine Office, and that they did this after Lauds. This took place before the actual *lectio divina* began. But during the hours of *lectio* they also committed passages from their reading to memory. This was a matter of course.

This exercise was called *meditatio,* which Leclercq defines as, "To pronounce the sacred words in order to retain them."[4]   The ancient Jews read the Scriptures aloud and as they read they memorized. The Hebrew word *hagah* means to murmur, to speak softly, which word St. Jerome translated by *meditari* in his Latin version of the Bible. So in Psalm 1, the person who "meditates" on God's law "day and night" is actually reciting the law from memory; the "mouth of the just man" which "meditabitur sapientiam" ("meditates wisdom") is reciting the wisdom of God as revealed in his word (Ps. 37:30). Because of this translation *meditatio* has acquired this particular biblical meaning of memorizing texts through listening to oneself reciting them.

Abbot Nesteros told Cassian, "Give yourself over assiduously, or rather continuously, to sacred reading, until continual meditation [*meditatio*] fills your heart, and fashions you so to speak after its own likeness.... The whole series of the Holy Scriptures should be diligently committed to memory and ceaselessly repeated."[5] So the Benedictine, in his *lectio divina,* learned what he read through hearing it. This is the usual way a person memorizes anything. *Lectio divina* was not "speed reading." The monk read aloud slowly, and took into his memory at least the essentials. When he found a text that struck him particularly, and wanted to learn it verbatim, he stopped and repeated it until he knew it by heart. This, and many other texts, were the ones that he kept, like Mary, in his heart, repeating them often to himself until they became part of him.

The text was held by the memory and, to be Jungian, went into the unconscious, where it went to work. It was the "seed that grows in silence," acting on its own, making the person into what it means. The Word of God has a power of its own. It goes out from God and does not return to him without results (cf. Is. 55:10-11). So it was a very good thing to have a memory and an unconscious well-stocked with God's word. This is what Abbot Nesteros meant when he spoke about "continual meditation" fashioning the monk "after its own likeness." So you can see the *meditatio* was a monastic way to that monastic goal, purity of heart.

But what about meditation in the non-biblical sense? Did a monk merely read aloud and memorize? No, of course not. Recall that we have been looking at two processes that formed the basic procedure for the early monk's *lectio divina*: reading aloud and memorizing. Of course they thought, and they also prayed. Anyone who read and memorized was naturally going to think and pray.

Meditatio, in its classical use, means a deep study, thinking out a subject. We will ask a person who is lost in thought what he is meditating on. A monk could meditate in this sense as soon as he began to read. For example, he was not going to get very far into an epistle of St. Paul without stopping to think. So *lectio* included thinking, even much and hard thinking.

As the monk pronounced the words aloud he could hear new meanings, meanings that he didn't get when he was thinking silently. By pronouncing the words he was, as it were, tasting them, and, as we do when we are tasting some new culinary creation, trying to determine what were the "ingredients." In this way the monk heard the deeper meaning of the text, its fuller sense. Of course, this was the Holy Spirit speaking in the word he inspired because, after all, the monk was listening to God.

The study of a text in *lectio divina*, pursuing its meaning, was not done for the sake of knowing about God, but of knowing God by experience, contacting him in his word. The monk did not seek for information as such but for Understanding, that knowledge of Revelation that is the gift of the Holy Spirit. Understanding in this sense is indeed one of the ends of *lectio divina*. But it results not so much in new facts learned as in that faith that is a share in God's own knowledge of himself, and it leads of itself to prayer. True, the ultimate purpose of *lectio divina* is going to God in prayer, but prayer which is stimulated by one's understanding of God.

As in the case of thinking, our monastic ancestors might pray as soon as they began to read. They knew what the exercise was for; they had a unified grasp of *lectio divina*, as they had of their life, and did not think of doing it in steps. Just hearing a text could start them off with pure prayer, unreasoned and spontaneous prayer, particularly a text that struck them forcibly and that they wanted to keep in their heart. Listening to it as they repeated it stimulated prayer. And listening to themselves read they had the sensation and the conviction through faith that they were listening to God, and of course they responded from the heart.

So Benedictines from the beginning into the Middle Ages did have a certain procedure in their *lectio divina*, almost amounting to a method, but a procedure in which they enjoyed the greatest liberty. Granted the fact that they read aloud, the rest followed in a natural way.

Guigo the Carthusian, who died in 1188, has left us a beautiful summary of the practice of monastic *lectio divina*. He wrote: "It is as the Lord says: 'Seek and you shall find; knock and it shall be opened to you' (Mt. 7:7). Seek in reading, and you will find in meditating; knock in praying, and you shall enter through contemplation." [6]

Although he seems to present us with steps, they are rather requisites and prerequisites, or elements. He says that "reading, meditation, prayer, and contemplation are so closely linked and so designed to be of mutual assistance that the first two are of little or no value without the latter. And these last two can rarely, if ever at all, be attained without the first two."[7]

Reading, thinking, memorizing, praying, these are elements of *lectio divina*. As to Guigo's *contemplation*, this is something that is up to God. This is God-given knowledge of himself, or of the text, or awareness of his presence, or infused love, or all of these together. The person does what *he* can do, and God does what *He* can do. Maybe God does not will to do anything. Contemplation is a gift, a grace. The monastic continues to do what he can do, and hopes and loves. "Lord, I long to see your face!" "Lord, that I may see!" Prayer, then, was really the heart and end of *lectio divina*, prayer that was the experience of God.

In light of the above we can conclude that *lectio divina* was what we call today *mental prayer*. It certainly must be considered as periods of prayer rather than of reading.

Benedictines have to read for information, for facts. They may have to read the Bible, the Fathers, and spiritual classics for this purpose. The priest-monk needs material for his homilies; the teacher, for theology and Scripture classes. That is all good and necessary. But this kind of reading must not be a substitute for *lectio divina*, even though the matter is definitely "divina." When we read the sermons and homilies of the Church Fathers we get the clear impression that they were the by-products of these men's *lectio divina*, rather than the products of their sermon preparation. And as to class preparation, theology teachers have to remember that theology has to be a *theologia mentis et cordis*—one has to reach the heart as well as the mind.

Now for the question that has been in the air during these pages— "What about Benedictines *today?*" This question actually includes three others:

1. Can today's Benedictine spend all that time on *lectio divina?*
2. Is he confined to reading only the Bible and the Church Fathers?
3. Must he read aloud and memorize?

As to Question 1: Obviously the contemporary Benedictine who works in a school, or in some form of pastoral and apostolic ministry, would find St. Benedict's minimum of two hours very difficult, and even impossible. Monastic work hasn't changed as to its elements but it certainly has as to its extent. All types of work and administration have become complex; activities can loom in frightening importance. Organization tries to hold it all together, and meetings, the lifeblood of organization, sap what vitality the monk has left. (One monk in such a situation said, "To Jesus through meetings.")

St. Benedict, at the beginning of Chapter 48, states the position of *lectio divina*. The monk's day, apart from the Office (and Mass), meals and sleep, consists of work and *lectio divina*. It is really on a par with work. It is a monastic essential, therefore it is important to the monastic. We have seen that it provides a means for his daily seeking and enjoying union with God. Without it could he go to Jesus through meetings or through anything else?

Lectio divina is definitely a part of the Benedictine way for the Benedictine. What should the busy monk do about it? First, if he has to, he should reorientate himself as to its importance. He must think of it as recreation, not as an obligatory exercise. He must look forward to it as a time to be simply with God. Second, he should do what he can. Here he must be both prudent and honest. He may have to rearrange his personal schedule, he must face the fact that he will not always enjoy the luxury of having a whole hour for his *lectio*. He may have only a half-hour, or twenty minutes. During the day he may have in-between times, intervals, when normally he would have a cup of coffee, or worry, putter, or browse. He can use these intervals. Blessed Alcuin, writing to some monks in the ninth century, said in effect that they should have in their hands at all times either a shovel or a book.

When the monk adds up these intervals in his day, plus a larger space in the early morning, and another at night, he will find that he can usually devote two hours a day to *lectio*. These times will definitely help continuous prayer, and when he puts everything together he will happily discover that the Benedictine life can be contemplative.

As to Question 2: Is the Benedictine confined for *lectio* to the Bible and the Church Fathers? I don't think that anyone is questioning reading the Bible but rather the amount of time to be spent on it. It is impossible to lay down quantitative rules for others. I believe that the Bible is the Benedictine's first book, and that his right attitude toward it is going to determine how much time he spends on it.

St. Benedict's list can certainly be extended to include the Doctors of the Church and other spiritual books that are regarded as classics. These latter are well-loved works not only of saints but also of other holy people through whom we can believe that God is speaking. Thus St. Benedict's two criteria for non-biblical authors—holy and catholic (ch. 73) can be satisfied.

Question 3: Must today's Benedictine read aloud as his ancestors did? If he is doing it only because his ancestors did, then no; but if he's reading aloud because his ancestors were on to a good thing, then yes. We're not treating here of some outmoded way of doing something but of reading aloud which, on occasion, many people do. We read aloud to ourselves when we want to understand a passage and we need also to hear it. We do the same in memorizing a passage. In reading the

Bible for *lectio divina* reading aloud is a great help. We seem to get more meanings that the eye would scan over. The rule here is, do what helps *you*. At least it will slow you down, and it is a help to attention and concentration.

As to memorizing, actually we can't do enough of it. It is a good and helpful practice for all of the reasons already given in this chapter, and nothing more need be said about it.

This, then, is St. Benedict's *lectio divina*, the same today as it was in his day. It is the only form of non-liturgical prayer that he legislates periods for.

*   *   *

Now we must have a longer look at the qualities of prayer, already mentioned earlier in this chapter. St. Benedict says in Chapter 20 of his Rule that prayer should be *pure*. Commentators on the Rule are quite definite that the adjective is not a random choice but a technical term and indicates a degree of prayer described by Abbot Isaac in Cassian's *Conferences* IX and X, and called by him *pure prayer*. Hence St. Benedict's *pura oratio*. They have good reason to so conclude and it is best to concur with their conclusion.

Abbot Cuthbert Butler in his *Benedictine Monachism*, first published in 1919, said *Conferences* IX and X, which are both on the subject of prayer, provided St. Benedict with his "manual" of prayer.[8]

Pure prayer according to Abbot Isaac is nothing less than what spiritual theology terms infused contemplation. It is therefore prayer that is given to a person by God, not prayer that he, himself, makes. It is his prayer in that his will, as a result of God's giving, goes out to God and he gives himself totally to Him. Abbot Isaac says that this prayer transcends human thought and conscious words. What the person says to God at this time he cannot always remember afterward. Sometimes, in this prayer, a person will shout for joy: "But sometimes the mind hides itself in complete silence within the secrets of a profound quiet, so that the amazement of a *sudden illumination* chokes all sounds of words and the overawed spirit either keeps all its feelings to itself or loses them and pours forth its desires to God with groanings that cannot be uttered."[9] (The italics are mine.)

Pure prayer is the prayer that St. Anthony of the Desert was talking about when he said: "That is not a perfect prayer wherein a monk understands himself and the words which he prays."[10]

Abbot Isaac uses Christ's Transfiguration before Peter, James, and John as an example of what pure prayer is,[11] and *pure* prayer is equated in Cassian with *fervent* prayer and *ardent* prayer. What Abbot Isaac is saying is that *pure* prayer is *all* prayer, not compounded with something else. To be able to throw ourselves into prayer that is totally outgoing to God with no, as St. Francis de Sales would say, "return on self," requires a special grace. Elsewhere Isaac speaks of a pure conscious, a pure mind, and purity of heart. When we put together all of his uses of *pure* we conclude that *pure prayer* is a gift from God that is given to a person who wants God alone. He desires only God, sees only God, thinks only God, and his conscience assures him that this is so.

One time when I was giving a retreat in a certain convent one of the Sisters came in for a talk. When she was leaving she said that she was going to chapel to contemplate. I said to her, "Good luck!" Infused contemplation, or pure prayer, cannot be "turned on." Techniques will not produce it. They can help, and they can serve as a certain method of preparation; but the real preparation has to be purity of heart, wanting and seeking God alone, and no techniques can substitute for that. The Benedictine way is simply to live the life. There are occasions that God uses to give this prayer, such as a psalm verse during the Divine Office, a sentence from a reading at Mass, or something that someone says that strikes one. These are springboards into the prayer that God is waiting to give.

A very big element in purity of heart is the person's desire for God alone and not for what he gives. This should be obvious from our experience of human love. To love another for his gifts is not true love. This is the love of the very young—and not always so very young— children who want their grandparents to come for Christmas because they bring them presents. We are dealing with almighty God who knows the human heart. If we go to prayer mainly because we look for the enjoyment that infused contemplation gives us we're not going to get it. Oh, maybe in the beginning of our search for God he will give this joy to us, but he is only showing us what he has in store for us.

Searching for him in dryness and perseverance is a test of whether we want him alone, and it's a good way for true love of God to be born and to grow.

Benedictines do not hurry. This is part of our way. Time we have. We do not look for instant results. We absorb this mentality from the very monastery we live in. This is not easy to do if our monastery was founded in 1947, but when we live in one that was first begun in 1155, we soak in the timelessness with the air we breathe. In fact the air is actually an atmosphere that is part chemical and part historical. And when we walk down great vaulted and stone-paved corridors, we see our monastic ancestors walking ahead of us along the same stones to the church for Matins in the very early hours of the new day, and we realize that we are part of one ageless moral person, and self and its progress don't seem as important as before.

What looms as important is that we seek God, as did these old monks, through icy corridors and icier churches, and not in deciding that *today* we are going to pass from "the prayer of forced acts" to "the prayer of simplicity."

Benedictines have never been too introspective, too concerned with self, because they are God-centered, Christ-centered. While they keep guard over their thoughts and actions, not only daily but even hourly, they do not keep their gaze fixed on themselves and their perfection but on Christ. Slowly, gradually, the Holy Spirit is making them into Christ.

St. Benedict seems to take it for granted that his monks will practice pure prayer—"Prayer should be short and pure" (ch. 20). And those who are truly seeking God do, although they may not be conscious of it. If you were to ask a busy monk or nun, "Do you practice pure prayer?" he or she may not know what to say and may leave you with a very unsatisfactory answer. But if you could observe that same monk or nun before the Blessed Sacrament, after their busy day, you would have your answer. The Benedictine simply enters and simply prays (ch. 52).

In the same Chapter 52 St. Benedict says that the monk should pray "with tears and heartfelt devotion." "Heartfelt devotion" translates *intentione cordis,* which is usually rendered by "purity of devotion." Actually this latter is the better translation because literally it means "the direction of the heart." The heart, that is the person's deepest desire, ought to be directed totally to God, he should really desire God alone. In other words, he should pray with purity of heart. This fact we have already seen.[12]

As to praying "with tears," St. Benedict means just what he says. According to Abbot Isaac tears can flow spontaneously for a number of reasons. The monk may be overcome with sorrow at the thought of his sins and failures. He may weep for joy when God lets him realize His presence. Or he may weep for others, for their hardness of heart, or for the sufferings of those who are being persecuted for their Faith.[13]

Praying with tears is good; it makes use of the body. We certainly make use of the body in liturgical prayer by means of gestures and movements; but in private prayer we must not be afraid to pray with our whole self, "flesh, soul, and spirit." Emotions can help, and we should stir them up as St. Paul tells us to stir up our faith. But emotions are psycho-physical and sometimes the body cannot be stirred up. Sickness, weather, dryness that we can't irrigate, may leave us depending totally on the will. But we should try to make use of the emotions because the will is often moved by them, and it's better to live by the whole person than by hanging on by the naked will alone. God wills us to live as a whole person.

If he is going to take us "out of the body," as it were, as he did St. Paul, and give us the prayer that is beyond images, beyond thought, we must remember that *he* is doing this. *We* have to pray as *we* can. When he takes over, then we enter his mode of existence and pray the prayer that *he* gives.

So let's not look down on praying with tears as something that "nice people" don't do. This is not something cultural, but something natural, and grace is not built on non-nature. "Nice people" are missing out not only on a lot of fun, but also on a lot of prayer!

What St. Benedict says that prayer should be, certainly applies to *lectio divina*—the periods of private prayer *par excellence*. These are really the times to pray with the whole self, with intentness of the heart on God, seeking, finding, knocking, and letting God open the door to contemplation.

NOTES

[1]Cf. *RB*, ch. 73. For Tradition as revelation, cf. *Dogmatic Constitution on Divine Revelation*, in *The Sixteen Documents of Vatican II* (Boston: Daughters of St. Paul, n. d.), pp. 380-381.

[2]Cf. *RB 1980*, pp. 467ff.

[3](New York: Mentor Omega Books, 1962), p. 24.

[4]*Ibid.*, p. 25.

[5]Cassian, *Conferences*, p. 440, First Conference of Abbot Nesteros, ch. 10.

[6]In Maurus Wolter, OSB, *The Principles of Monasticism* (St. Louis: B. Herder Book Co., 1962), p. 215.

[7]*Ibid.*

[8](London: Longmans, Green and Co., 1919), p. 78.

[9]*Conferences*, IX, p. 396. *Conferences* IX and X should be read, pp. 387-409. I am giving here the barest summary.

[10]*Ibid.*, p. 398.

[11]*Ibid.*, X, p. 403.

[12]Cf. Cassian, *Conferences*, IX, ch. 6, p. 390; ch. 12, p. 391.

[13]Cf. *ibid.*, IX, ch. 29, p. 397.

IV
Community

THE BENEDICTINE'S SEARCH FOR GOD is personal, as is his union with Him. We have seen thus far that monks and nuns pursue God in continual prayer, and in definite periods of prayer, particularly in *lectio divina*. These pursuits are personal, and they are absolutely necessary to one who wants only God. We have considered them first, before taking up such other monastic elements as Community and the *Opus Dei*, because they rank first in importance to the individual.

A monastic who is not concerned with working at continual prayer or *lectio divina* is not going to be an authentic community person. He may be considered to be a "good mixer," a good worker, a "real acquisition," but a Benedictine community is not a club, a task force, or a faculty house. If an individual is not eager for personal prayer, liturgical prayer will settle into mere ritual, and even into a performance. Participation must come from the heart that wants God alone.

Another reason for considering personal prayer first is that superiors can, by simply scanning the choir stalls, tell who is and who isn't present for the Divine Office, but there exists no such method of determining who is or who isn't practicing personal private prayer. As a result, the monk can ease up on the latter, even though working at a great fidelity to choir attendance; and eventually he wonders why he isn't "getting anything out of" the Office and, I daresay, the Mass.

So now we can consider the Benedictine in his situation, in his community. Much has been written in recent years on the subject of community, ranging from studies of New Testament *koinonia* to the application of findings of psychology and sociology. In this chapter we shall only look at what St. Benedict has to say about community, and we shall see that he is a master of psychology and sociology.

In the first chapter of his Rule, St. Benedict states that there are two kinds of authentic monks: cenobites and hermits. He is writing his Rule for cenobites,[1] who "no longer live by their own judgment, giving in to their whims and appetites; rather they walk according to another's decisions and directions, choosing to live in monasteries and to have an abbot over them" (*RB 1980* 5, 12).

Why would somebody prefer to live in a monastery under the surveillance and guidance of an abbot, obeying the will of another, and, unless he was an outright gregarious extrovert, want to live at very close range with a number of others whom he didn't choose, when he could have a nice cozy little place of his own and still be considered a monk? Simply because the cenobitic life has advantages for the Christian who is truly seeking God. St. Benedict calls the cenobite *fortissimum genus* (ch. 1), which we can translate as *the rugged kind*. And even though a person who enters a monastery today is a product of our comfort-crazed culture—abhorring suffering as the ultimate evil—if he has a good will and pure intention, by God's grace and the cenobitic life, he will emerge as rugged.

What is the advantage of this ruggedness? St. Benedict says that a monk may become a hermit, but only after long training in the monastery: "Thanks to the help and guidance of many, they are now trained to fight against the devil. They have built up their strength and go from the battleline in the ranks of their brothers to the single combat of the desert. Self-reliant now, without the support of another, they are ready with God's help to grapple single-handed with the vices of body and mind" (*RB 1980* 1, 4-5).

A Benedictine has to be a fighter. In his seeking God he will meet obstacles—dragons, if you like. One of these will be Satan, but others he will be surprised to discover are within himself: pride, sensuality, possessiveness. He learns how to conquer these obstacles from the guidance of the community, from their example, and from their encouragement. He learns how to stand on the front line and to self-reliantly smite the worst dragon of all, The Terrible Importance of *Me*.

A monastery, according to St. Benedict, is going to contain strong and weak. He presumes this fact (cf. ch. 64). Thank God for the strong because they encourage the weak, beginning with the crucial event of the day, getting up in the morning (cf. ch. 22). A Benedictine is one who seeks God along with the help of his community; and being part of the community, he helps the others to the same end.

St. Benedict calls his community "a school of the Lord's service" (Prologue). It is a school in which the superior, not the disciple, is the teacher: "Speaking and teaching are the master's task; the disciple is to be silent and to listen" (*RB 1980* 6, 6). St. Benedict's abbot is not primarily an executive but a teacher, because the monastery is not primarily a corporation but a school where the monks learn every day of their lives how to serve God. It is really a trade school because for this service the monks learn how to skillfully use seventy-four tools, "the tools of the spiritual craft" (ch. 4): "The workshop where we are to toil faithfully at all these tasks is the enclosure of the monastery and stability in the community" (*RB 1980* 4, 78).

All of this would be advantage enough in belonging to a Benedictine community, but the help of many companions in the pursuit of God derives from a deeper level of meaning. In St. Benedict's mind his monastery is the Church. God calls a person to the monastic life not as to something *outré* or "freakish" but to the full development of the essential Christian life. In a Benedictine monastery people strive to live the fullness of the life that Christ came to give. Therefore St. Benedict's monastery is to be the ideal Church, the Mystical Body of Christ in full force.

The reason why his monks are the *fortissimum genus*, is that they vow with an adult commitment to do that which Baptism did for them. A Christian by his baptism is consecrated to God to live Christ's life perfectly, but he usually does so in the married state, owning material possessions, and exercising his free will over a wide area. The cenobite gives to God these three natural rights, that he or she may go to God naked and alone. Unlike a married person the cenobite goes to God not *through* a spouse, but *with* other like-minded seekers.

Such a life is both solitary and social and definitely that of the Church. Cenobites live out together the life of Christ and exemplify that life to the whole of society and particularly to the whole Church. The monastery is the image of what the Church should be and essentially is.

Cassian says that St. Mark brought the life of the primitive Christians in Jerusalem to Alexandria when he established the Church there. We are all familiar with the descriptions in the Acts of the Apostles of the way the first Christians lived: "And they devoted themselves to the Apostles' teaching and fellowship, to the breaking of bread and the prayers" (2:42); "And all who believed were together and had all things in common; and they sold their possessions and goods and distributed them to all, as any had need" (2:44-45); "Now the company of those who believed were of one heart and soul, and no one said that any of the things which he possessed was his own, but they had everything in common" (4:32).

What St. Mark brought to Egypt may not look like the monastic life but it was simply the life of the early Church. When the Egyptians no longer lived this perfect quasi-cenobitical life, the tradition remained and with it the understanding of what the Christian life actually is. The individuals who wished to devote themselves to it, such as St. Anthony, the father of monks, were not doing something "super-Christian" but simply Christian. The monastic life in its origins, then, was the continuation of the life of the early Church.[2]

St. Benedict calls his monastery "the house of God" (chs. 31, 53, 64), and thus he is calling it the Church. This is rather obvious. In the Old Testament the temple was called "the house of God" and "the house of the Lord." It, together with the hill it stood on, Sion, was a symbol for the whole nation of the People of God, as also was Jerusalem, the city of the temple. Christ called the temple "my Father's house" (Lk. 2:49; Jn. 2:16). But in his role of fulfilling the Old Testament he revealed what this house of God really was meant to be: his Body. "Destroy this temple, and in three days I will raise it up.... But he spoke of the temple of his body" (Jn. 2:19, 21). According to St. Paul the Church is the Body of Christ, the extension in time and space of that same suffering and glorified Body.[3]

St. Benedict also calls his monks a *flock* (chs. 2, 27, 28, 63, 64). He means by this term a flock of sheep, and the abbot is the shepherd (ch. 2). But what at first might strike one as a rather distressing metaphor becomes clear when we read in Chapter 27 that the abbot is "to imitate the loving example of the Good Shepherd," and therefore we realize that shepherd and flock are none other than Christ and his Church. Our Lord did not choose sheep to symbolize his followers because they are rather mindless animals, placidly bleating in gregarious content, but because of the relationship that existed between the Palestinian shepherd and his sheep, something that his hearers would understand. The tenth chapter of St. John's Gospel expresses it beautifully: "I am the Good Shepherd. The Good Shepherd lays down his life for the sheep.... I know my own and my own know me, as the Father knows me and I know the Father.... He who enters by the door is the shepherd of the sheep.... The sheep hear his voice, and he calls his own sheep by name and leads them out." Therefore the abbot or abbess is to hold the place of Christ for the community (ch. 2).

To see the abbot as Christ is a function of the eyes of faith. The same eyes must see the community as Church. Any secularizing or purely humanizing of the community will weaken the monks' supernatural view of their abbot. A monastery that sees itself primarily as a place where a group of busy people resides and does some praying together will tend to take its abbot as the chairman of the board.

St. Benedict says that the reason why the head of the monastery is called *abbot* derives from St. Paul: "You have received the spirit of adoption of sons by which we exclaim, *abba*, father" (Rm. 8:15; ch, 2). *Abba*, he says, is a title of Christ, therefore the *abba* of the monastery takes Christ's position or role. There are several theologies contained in St. Benedict's several sentences, and I can only summarize.

First is "the spirit of adoption of sons" (Romans 8 should be read as a whole): The purpose of the Church is to give the life that Christ came to merit and to give. Actually this life is the Holy Spirit. At his death he bowed his head and handed over the Spirit (Jn. 19:30). The Spirit puts each baptized person in Christ's Body, which is the Church. Since the Christian is now *in* Christ, who is the Son of God by *nature*, he becomes the *adopted* child of God.

Second, as to *abba*: this, in the Gospels and St. Paul's epistles, is how Christ addressed God the Father. It is an Aramaic word and has an affectionate ring to it that can be translated by "daddy." But Christ is God the Son; how can St. Benedict call it a title of Christ?

Recall that Christ said to Philip, "He who has seen me has seen the Father; how can you say, 'Show us the Father'? Do you not believe that I am in the Father and the Father in me?" (Jn. 14:9-10). He is the image of the invisible God (Col. 1:15), the visible way to the Father (Jn. 14:6). The Father sent him to merit our forgiveness and the gift of the Holy Spirit. Because of his mediation he is for us a father, he is the source for us of these good things that flow to us from his atoning death. The Father sent him to reveal all truth, so as father he teaches us and rears us. The adopted children are able rightfully to call God their Father because they are able first to call Christ by this title, Christ who merited for them this right.

All this is a little background for calling the superior of the monastery *abbot* (or abbess), and meaning thereby *Christ*. It is another way of saying that St. Benedict envisioned his monastery as the Church with the guiding, teaching Christ present as the abbot.

So the greatest advantage of the Benedictine cenobitical life comes from the fact that the Benedictine monastery is the Church for its members.[4] Hence, helping each other seek God alone cannot consist simply in a smile and a "How are you?" or regaling the confrères at recreation with a witty *raconte*. Of course we must smile and inquire and regale but that is not enough. Benedictines have to be pipelines of the Holy Spirit for each other. What the Church is about is giving the Holy Spirit, and Benedictines are Church. Relationships have to be basically sacramental.

A cursory reading of the Rule leaves one with the strong impression that a Benedictine community consists of people with a variety of differences. One sees this at first in Chapter 2, on the qualities of the abbot. The abbot has accepted the difficult task of ruling human beings and "serving a variety of temperaments." One thinks immediately of a house full of mixed cholerics, phlegmatics, sanguines, and melancholics! The word that *temperaments* translates is *moribus*. One edition of the Rule translates it as *dispositions*. The word itself can mean *customs, ways*, as in "set in his ways." In any case what St. Benedict is telling his abbot is that he can expect to face a group of individuals who are not only different from each other, but who have acquired through the years their own peculiar habits and ways of doing things, as well as ways of reacting.

An English abbot in a retreat conference broke up our community when he said, "A Benedictine monastery is like a grain of mustard seed, which grows into a good-sized tree and some mighty strange birds come and nest in its branches."

Benedictines are fond of saying that each monastery has its own family traits, and that they can pretty well tell who comes from which monastery because of these. I am sure that this is so, because a close-knit group of people is going to acquire not only an *esprit de corps* but also a common way of viewing what is important, and of deciding what is not. But what a Benedictine monastery should not become is a collection of people who are all of the same type. "Fitting in" is a good criterion of a vocation to a particular house, but it should never mean fitting in with similarities of tastes. A monastery that can be described as one large clique is doomed to break into rival cliques when tastes change. A candidate should not be rejected because "he is not our type."

St. Benedict expects a "mixed bag," and that, through the ages, is what a healthy Benedictine monastery has always been. Imagine a group of people who are of various ethnic backgrounds, various races, consisting of strong cholerics, cheerful sanguines, slow phlegmatics, retiring melancholics, Cubs fans, and even, God forbid, baseball-haters, rabid Republicans, vocal Democrats, "old school ties" and non-school-non-ties, musicians and the tone deaf, and you have the raw material for a promising Benedictine monastery. Add difference in ages, and difference in responsiveness to God's grace, plus attitudes toward fresh air, and you begin to get the true picture of what St. Benedict expects, and, I'm sure, wants. What gets all of these variegated people together is God's call to each one to seek union with him in this particular monastery; what keeps them together is their pursuit of this union. And so, "whether slave or free," St. Benedict quotes St. Paul, "we are all one in Christ" (Ch. 2).

Different though monastics be, they come to acquire a common mentality, a way of looking at the essentials of their life that I have called the Benedictine Way. This common mentality comes from this variety of personalities, each with his own particular mentality, background and experiences, applied to living the Rule of St. Benedict. That it is at all achieved—and it is—is due to God's grace and the genius of the Rule.

How can this unity of differences help them all to the one end of union with God? How does community work for Benedictines?

First of all, by the monks' and nuns' realizing, and accepting, that they are all different. St. Benedict is certainly realistic enough about this. He says that monks should support "with the greatest patience one another's weaknesses of body or behavior" (ch. 72). Different people with different health problems and/or personality traits must be borne "with the *greatest* patience." But when the monk "sees the beam in his own eye," then Benedictine community life can begin.

After this initial recognition Benedictines must keep firmly and ever in mind that they all have come together for only one purpose; and even though in some this may seem doubtful, it is true. (One should not be too quick to judge a "doubtful case." Maybe the doubtful cases are the ones who have really found God.) From here on the person must keep his viewpoint supernatural and remember that the monastery is "the house of God," the Church, the Body of Christ, in whom all of these individuals are adopted children of God the Father. The power of the house is the power that drove Christ—the Holy Spirit. "All this the Lord will by the Holy Spirit graciously manifest in his workman" (*RB 1980* 7, 70). Therefore the members of the community must treat each other with reverence. If the tools and utensils of the monastery are sacred because they are used in the service of God in the house of God, all the more so are the monks and nuns who use them and whose vocation and presence are the very reason why the place and things are sacred (cf. ch. 31).

"They should each try to be the first to show respect to the other," St. Benedict quotes Romans 12:10 (ch. 72). Benedictines reverence each other as Christ. This supernatural attitude towards each member of the community dictates the way they address each other: the juniors call the seniors *Nonnus* and seniors call the juniors *Brother. Nonnus*, a word of Egyptian origin, is untranslatable. It was a word of address used for older men, and always conveyed the idea of respect. Italians today call their grandfather *Nonno*.[5] The terms *Brother* and *Nonnus* denote family, and for Benedictines their use of these is an act of faith in the fact of their supernatural family (cf. ch. 63).

We note in the Rule that St. Benedict expects a great reverence for the seniors (ch. 63). Monks must obey the abbot and the other superiors, that is obvious, but St. Benedict says, "in every other instance younger monks should obey their seniors with all love and concern" (ch. 71). Futhermore, if a monk "gets the impression that one of his seniors is angry or disturbed with him, however slightly, he must, then and there without delay, cast himself on the ground at the other's feet to make satisfaction, and lie there until the disturbance is calmed by a blessing." Then he adds, "anyone who refuses to do this should be subjected to corporal punishment or, if he is stubborn, should be expelled from the monastery" (ch. 71).

Hardly a youth culture! And yet, not necessarily one weighted in favor of the old: "Absolutely nowhere shall age automatically determine rank. Remember that Samuel and Daniel were still boys when they judged their elders" (ch. 63). The abbot can promote a monk because of the worthiness of his life, but normally all hold rank according to the time they entered the monastery. It is possible for a thirty-year old to be senior in rank to a newcomer of fifty. But St. Benedict's seniors are the more or less rugged veterans, seniors in the sense that they have been around for a long time and have helped form the customs and the spirit of the house. These are the ones who should have earned the paternal reverence shown them.

The seniors, St. Benedict says, should love the juniors (chs. 72; 4:71). This love is not to be of the emotional kind because he actually wants all the monks to love each other with the chaste love of brotherhood (cf. ch. 72). The Latin word here for love is *caritas*, which is the love that gives even though the other fails to give back, disinterested love, love without thought of return. This kind of love can be difficult because it does not necessarily have the help and consolation of the emotion of love. Yet this is why Benedictines are able to cope with each other's peculiarities, that they can have compassion for the elderly and for the demanding sick, and the gaucheries of the newcomers. Because they are conscious of the supernatural character of their brotherhood, they willingly cooperate with each other.

This brings us to mutual obedience. "Obedience is a blessing to be shown by all, not only to the abbot but also to one another as brothers, since we know that it is by this way of obedience that we go to God" (ch. 71)..."earnestly competing in obedience to one another" (ch. 72). The reason for this mutual obedience is that a monk should be concerned for others, not himself. "No one is to pursue what he judges better for himself, but instead, what he judges better for somone else" (*RB* 72, 7). A Benedictine is not a soul-searching introspective type who is continually concerned about his needs. Usually he is too busy to think about himself, and in any case he has learned to find God not only in God's will but also in his brothers and sisters. His concern is, "What do *you* need?" He sees the brethren as Christ: lonely, tired, frustrated, even discouraged.

A Benedictine can pride himself on only one thing—on being a good community person; and this is easy to determine—whether he is consistently thoughtful of others. St. Benedict can translate this thoughtfulness into care that one does not disturb others, for example, by one's distracting mannerisms in church, and by being noisy when another monk is trying to sleep (chs. 48 and 52). A true Benedictine defines community as service to others. (Father Choleric, who has to go out for a 6:30 A.M. Mass in the nearby city says, "Community is filling the gas tank when you bring the car back on empty.") It is possible that a monk may be a model of regularity and hard work and not be a good community person because he is not thoughtful of others.

A monastery trains and educates its members so that they can share in the community works. The purpose of such education can never be the enrichment and development of the person solely for his own advantage. Enriched and developed he may well be, but he is expected to give what he has become for the good of the community. Someone who uses the monastery as a stepping stone to his personal ambitions has no vocation to be a Benedictine.

A Benedictine community works not only because the monks and nuns are all united in their one purpose and therefore in their supernatural attitude toward their life, but also because they are making an honest effort to be humble. When you have a group of people all scrambling for the last place, you have a smooth running community. We will take a good look at this fundamental virtue in Chapter 6.

Another help is St. Benedict's insistence on order. Nothing is left to personal whims, nothing is spontaneous. The daily life of the monastery proceeds according to a regular horarium. It flows between well-defined banks. The *Opus Dei,* work, *lectio,* meals, sleep: all occur at fixed times. The only thing that changes is the sun, and these day-to-day activities depend on the amount of daylight. Their times may change seasonally, but within the seasons they are fixed. As St. Benedict says, "so that everything may be done at the proper time" (ch. 47).

Officials are appointed by the abbot or abbess and these officials carry out their duties according to a regular order. Cooks, waiters, guest-master, porter, the one in charge of clothing, prefects, procurator, infirmarian, these all know what they have to do to make the monastery a place of peace. St. Benedict tells the procurator, "Necessary items are to be requested and given at the proper times, so that no one may be disquieted or distressed in the house of God" (ch. 31).

There it is, the one motive for it all: peace in the house of God. Everything must favor continual prayer and fraternal charity. These activities demand an atmosphere that favors prayer and that is free from the irritations that make charity difficult. One of our mottoes is *Pax,* and St. Benedict's insistence on order guarantees that at least the ambience of the place is that of peace.

The great calamity in Benedictine community life is excommunication. St. Benedict provides for this happening. What is this monastic excommunication? Exactly what the word says: putting an individual out of community life. He can be excluded partially or totally depending on the gravity of his offense. What kind of an offense would deserve excommunication? Disobedience and pride, but to the extent that a monk defies his superiors, holds stubbornly to his position, thus defying the Rule, which by his vows he has willingly accepted as his guide. St. Benedict adds murmuring, which in this case would be opposing authority by one's rebellious word behind authority's back (ch. 23). A monk who is guilty of this kind of conduct should be privately corrected twice, then, if he does not change his ways, be rebuked publicly. Only after that, if he clearly and openly despises the very foundations of the monastic life should he be excommunicated.

There are two kinds of excommunication. The lesser is called "exclusion from the common table," and means just that. The monk takes his meals alone at some other time. Also he takes no leading parts at the *Opus Dei*. The other kind is total excommunication, and is reserved for the apparently unrepentant. The person is excluded from the two great community places: the refectory and the church. No one may associate with him, except the abbot and mature, wise monks whom the abbot sends to talk to him (chs. 25, 27). Meanwhile abbot and community pray for his conversion. If he does not change his attitude and his ways, then he is dismissed from the monastery. As St. Benedict aptly puts it, quoting St. Paul, "If the unbeliever departs, let him depart" (ch. 28).

This kind of excommunication rarely occurs today. But there is a kind that does occur, and it is not always so rare. This is what we can call private or unofficial excommunication, not decreed by the abbot but done by a monk himself. An individual can take himself out of community, never eating at the common table and absenting himself from the *Opus Dei* and conventual Mass. I am not referring to those whose duties prevent their sharing in the community's meals and liturgical acts, but to those who create for themselves a personal schedule that excludes community functions. The community does not avoid them, but they avoid the community and live their own lives under the same roof as the others.

More common is a more subtle and less apparent form of excommunication—monks shunning other monks. Usually this is not done deliberately, and when the monks' attention is called to the fact, they are shocked to realize that they are doing this. But it happens, and usually to the shy, very quiet kind, those who "don't make waves." They are the ones who are never included in invitations, mainly because nobody thinks of them. And that is what is sad about it— nobody seems to be concerned or interested in them. They are the forgotten ones of the monastery.

There will always be those who don't seem to fit in. These have to be brought in. Many a "hidden gem" has been discovered in this way, sadly, later in the person's life, because he or she never had a chance to be heard and gave up trying.

Cliques are another form of excommunication. That fact is obvious. But again the formation of a clique can happen quite innocently. A group of monks or nuns may be engaged in the same work, and as is the case "in the world," those who work together play together.

Does all this mean that Benedictine community life is an exercise in continual and strenuous "togetherness"? God forbid! It is true that, in St. Benedict's time, monks slept in a common dormitory, but according to the standards of the Fathers of the Desert, the fact that the monks were able to sleep in a decent bed at all was quite a concession. Through the centuries Benedictines have acquired private rooms, or cells, where they have been able to enjoy some degree of solitude. As it has developed, it is reasonable to say that Benedictine life can be one of solitude in the context of community. *Balance* is the word, and the way to Benedictine balance is simply to live the life.

If cliques are to be avoided, what, then, about friendship? May monks and nuns have special friends? Friendship is a natural good, like eating and sleeping. One can overdo these latter activities, or "underdo" them, but they are not to be eliminated because of abuses either way. It is absolutely unnatural to dole out love in equal measure for all. To try to love everyone alike will turn the person into a machine. Christ had special friends—Lazarus for one, at whose tomb he could weep, even though he knew that in five minutes he was going to bring him back to life. No, here we are speaking of what older monks and nuns will recall as "particular friendships," which spiritual directors used to inveigh against. A "particular friendship" is one that is emotional, and the unspoken implication was always that it had a sexual basis. All special friendships between religious were discouraged because of the constant fear that they would develop into a "particular friendship." As a result many religious retired into their shells, crushing down their natural desire to love and be loved, substituting duty for love.

Such a mentality prevailed during the nineteenth century, when so many modern Congregations of men and women were founded, and persisted throughout the first half of this century. It all ended when religious discovered encounter groups, and reached out and touched in unfettered sensitivity.

But Benedictines, viewing all of this from the vantage point of centuries, must keep their heads and their balance. They should have the common sense to sense danger, as well as the sound and serene mentality that the life of the Rule engenders, to be able to perceive truth. The Benedictine mentality is objective. It can distinguish reasoning from rationalizing.

The Rule gives us two norms for a "safe" friendship:

1. To show the chaste love of brotherhood (ch. 72), and

2. "Every precaution must be taken that one monk does not presume in any circumstance to defend another in the monastery or to be his champion, even if they are related by the closest ties of blood" (ch. 69).

We can interpret this second norm as meaning that a friendship between two monks does not mean that they can stand apart from the others, pitted against the others, as if for combat, or as a tight little duo that excludes everyone else. Monastic friendship excludes no one, as it is ready to include everyone. When Father Choleric was younger he used to say, "Thank God we're not commanded to *like* everyone!" Now, wiser and mellower, he has come to realize that disliking others makes it very difficult for the Holy Spirit to infuse charity into a nonreceptive heart.

Benedictines are unique among religious in that every abbey and conventual priory is independent of every other. This means that each monastery is the Order of St. Benedict for its monks and nuns and, if it ceased to be, so would they as Benedictines. In America, the members of a community own their monastery as a corporation. This places a responsibility on each one. Not only is each monk or nun responsible for making objective and supernaturally motivated decisions in chapter meetings—meetings of all those who have made perpetual vows— but also each one is responsible for the progress and welfare of the house (cf. ch. 3).

St. Benedict lays down the principle, "All things should be the common possession of all" (ch. 33; cf. Acts 4:32). Benedictine poverty works two ways—individually the monastic is poor, corporately he may be rich. But he may not view the whole plant with smug proprietorship, seeing it as the means of supporting a life-style to which he is really not accustomed. Such was the view of monks of decadent periods in the history of the Order, whose monasteries today have to be owned and maintained by the State as national monuments and in which the present monks live as guests.

The contemporary monk and nun has to see the plant as *his* or *her* responsibility. It is easy to let the procurator worry about such items as electric bills and the cost of gasoline. It is easy to pass the buck to the superior. Other Orders can let provincial councils worry, or the General Council in Rome. Benedictines not so. Abbot and procurator are part of the home. A monastic has to maintain his home as a working son or daughter, not use it as a spoiled child.

Nor can he avoid responsibility for the spirit and tone of the house: "It's up to the abbot to see what's going on and to do something about it." That is an immature approach, for a responsible person will know that the spirit of the house is *his* concern. When you have a monastery in which each member is responsibly seeking God, then you will have a real Benedictine community, corporately seeking God, and the monastery will truly be the house of God and the gate of heaven.

NOTES

[1] *RB 1980*, ch. 1. The translation of the Rule in this chapter is usually that of *RB 1980*, Timothy Fry, OSB, ed.

[2] Cf. Cassian, *Institutes*, Bk II, Ch. 5, Gibson ed., pp. 206-207.

[3] Cf. 2 Cor. 6:16; Eph. 2:19-22.

[4] Cf. *Lumen Gentium, The Dogmatic Constitution on the Church*, Ch. 6, in *The Sixteen Documents of Vatican II* (Boston: Daughters of St. Paul, n.d.), pp. 158-162; and Claude J. Peifer, OSB, *Monastic Spirituality* (New York: Sheed and Ward, 1966), pp. 68-71.

[5] Cf. *RB 1980*, Mark Sheridan, OSB, "Monastic Terminology: Monk, Cenobite, Nun," p. 321.

V

The Opus Dei

BENEDICTINES ARE CHRISTIANS, and Christians form a one from many, a unity of diverse and varied people, the Body of Christ. Christians have a sense of solidarity. Common prayer is essential to Christianity: the individuals know that when they pray together they are reaching the Father through Christ and with him, because they are *in* him. They know that "where two or three are gathered in my name, there am I in the midst of them" (Mt. 18:20).

The Benedictine community is the Church for its monks and nuns, therefore Benedictines at common prayer are the one Church at prayer, reaching out beyond the group to include all the Church. Because the Church prays together so do the monks and nuns. With the first Church in Jerusalem they devote themselves "to the prayers" (cf. Acts 2:42). They pray with "one heart and soul" (Acts 4:32).

Opus Dei, the Work of God, is St. Benedict's term for this community prayer. It consists basically of the whole psalter, the 150 psalms, prayed throughout the course of one week, to which are added readings from the Bible and the Church Fathers, hymns, and prayers. St. Benedict distributes this prayer throughout the day and the night in what are called Hours. Out of the seventy-three chapters of the Rule, St. Benedict devotes eleven to the composition and distribution of the *Opus Dei* (*RB,* chs. 8-18).

Realistically *Opus Dei* should be translated Work *for* God, because that is how St. Benedict conceives it. The monastery is the house of God, therefore those who live in it owe God service.

The Benedictine monastery is "a school for the Lord's service" (*RB 1980,* Prol. 45). Therefore Benedictines owe God the service of their common prayer. St. Benedict says that "we satisfy our obligations of service" by the hours of the *Opus Dei* (*RB 1980* 16, 2). And "monks who in a week's time say less than the full psalter with the customary canticles betray extreme indolence and lack of devotion in their service" (*ibid.*, 18, 24). Prescribing how the monks are to pray the *Opus Dei* he quotes Psalm 2, "Serve the Lord with fear" (*ibid.*, 19, 3).

It is the superior's responsibility to give the signal for each Hour of the *Opus Dei.* And whoever reads or sings at this common prayer should do so with "humility, seriousness, and reverence" (*RB*, ch. 47). The Latin word that *reverence* translates is *tremore,* which adds a note of fearful trembling. The *Opus Dei* is a serious business, and St. Benedict does not want the monks to forget it because it is the service of almighty God. "On hearing the signal for an hour of the divine office, the monk will immediately set aside what he has in hand and go with utmost speed, yet with gravity and without giving occasion for frivolity" (*RB 1980* 43, 1-2). When the signal is given to get up in the morning the monks should "vie with one another in hastening to the Work of God, yet with all gravity and modesty" (*RB,* ch. 22).[1]

If the words "service" and "duty" sound rather onerous and unattractive, we have to investigate what this duty consists of. St. Benedict says "we satisfy our obligations of service at Lauds, Prime, Terce, Sext, None, Vespers and Compline," seven Hours, because "The Prophet says: *Seven times a day have I praised you*" (Ps. 119:164). And the reason for Matins—"The same Prophet says: *At midnight I arose to give you praise* (Ps. 119:62). Therefore, we should praise our Creator for his just judgments at these times: Lauds, Prime, Terce, Sext, None, Vespers, and Compline; and let us arise at night to give him praise" (*RB 1980,* 16).

So Benedictines' duty of service is actually to give God praise, which ought to be a pleasant task and one to which they should look forward. In their common prayer they join the angels in their praise of God. St. Benedict quotes Psalm 138: "*in the presence of the angels I will sing to you,*" and adds, "Let us consider, then, how we ought to behave in the presence of God and his angels" (*RB 1980* 19, 5-6). The *Opus Dei* takes the monks to heaven and their eternal occupation, hence it must be a joyful duty.

Praising God is telling Him about himself, and comes out of one's personal experience of God. The monks' common praise proceeds from their continual prayer, *lectio divina,* and other personal prayers. What they have learned of God in private they praise when they come together, and God will reveal more of himself during the Divine Office to those who are open to him. For St. Gertrude, one of our nuns, the words of the *Opus Dei* were doors through which she went to Christ. The Hours of the Office were mystical experiences for Gertrude.

What Benedictines primarily are telling God in their common praise is that He is God. Hence their praise is fundamentally adoration which, expressed externally, becomes worship. Monastics have to realize this fact. They come together at stated times during the day and night to give God the pure glory of adoration. This is objective prayer with nothing subjective about it, save the personal dispositions of each one. This variety of different individuals is united in the one work of adoring God with one voice.

The *Opus Dei* is the Benedictines' first work. St. Benedict says, "Nothing is to be preferred to the Work of God" (*RB 1980* 43, 3). But even if he hadn't made that famous statement, it would still necessarily have to be the primary occupation of monks and nuns because the search for God and union with him has to be their primary preoccupation. When we think about it, the *Opus Dei* results from the Christian's need to pray always, and a group of Christians who live together is necessarily going to pray together as much as it possibly can. So the *Opus Dei* is a Christian service before it is monastic.

Actually the *individual's* first work is to seek God by union with his will and by continual prayer. (This is the reason why I treated continual prayer first.) The *Opus Dei* as the *community's* first work flows from this seeking and gives expression to it. By its place and its prominence it makes the statement that the whole *raison d'être* of the monastery is union with God.

St. Benedict was not original in his determining upon eight Hours for the Divine Office, nor in his choice of names and times. He had his sources, but he was original in his use of these, e.g., in his arrangement of the psalms for each Hour, and in deciding that the night office should be in the early part of the day, after the monks had had their full sleep.

His sources for his arrangement of the *Opus Dei* were the practices of the monks of Egypt, Palestine, Mesopotamia, and elsewhere in the Middle East and Greece, the liturgies that had developed in cathedrals, and the customs of pre-existing and current European monasteries. An important source was the *Rule of the Master.*[2] Inspiring all of these various and widespread earlier groups was the custom of praying privately and publicly at stated times by the ordinary laity in the first three centuries. These men and women would pray not only in the morning, the evening, and at night, but also at the third, sixth, and ninth hours.[3]

What is the significance of the Hours of the *Opus Dei?* Vigils is the monks' prayer during the night. Its justification is simply the verse from Psalm 119: "Concerning Vigils, the same Prophet says: *At midnight I arose to give you praise. . . . Let us arise at night to give him praise*" (*RB 1980* 16, 4-5; Psalm 119:62). Back of this is the Saturday night vigil of the Desert Fathers, the Sunday morning vigil in cathedrals and other churches, and nightly vigils of continental monasteries. But for St. Benedict we must note that the monks pray vigils in the earliest hours of the new day for only one reason: that monks should praise God at night. The day is divided into seven prayer meetings, the night is also part of the twenty-four hour day and must have its Hour. His thinking is that monks owe God continuous praise, and, of course, the ideal of continual prayer forms the foundation of the whole *Opus Dei.* So, it is praise to God, "morning, noon, and night."

The times of the *Opus Dei* are determined by the sun, a very natural arrangement. We can see this when we read the hymns for most of the Hours in the old monastic Divine Office. This fact gives a natural significance to the Hours.

Lauds is the praise of God at dawn. The monks see the sun at this time as a symbol of God, and particularly of Christ. The hymn for Monday's Lauds begins with this beautiful verse:

Thou Brightness of the Father's ray,
True Light of light and Day of day,
Light's fountain and eternal spring,
Thou Morn, the morn illumining!

Prime, at sunrise, begins the work day. While Lauds is praise, Prime is more pragmatic—it gets the monks going. We can see this from the first verse of the hymn:

> Now that the daylight fills the sky,
> We lift our hearts to God on high,
> That he, in all we do or say,
> Would keep us free from harm today.

Terce, Sext, and None, the prayer of the third, sixth, and ninth hours, probably originated as prayers in the Jerusalem temple and in the synagogues. We read in Acts that Peter and John went up to the temple for the ninth hour of prayer (Acts 3:1). The early Church took over these prayer times because of their particular significance for Christians: Christ carried his cross at the third hour, was hung on it at the sixth, and died at the ninth; the Holy Spirit descended on the apostles at the third hour; at the sixth hour Peter had his symbolic dream about the Gentiles, and at "the ninth hour of prayer" an angel appeared to the Gentile, Cornelius, telling him to send for Peter to baptize him and his household (cf. Acts 10:3-48).

Vespers is the hour of praise at sunset, and also derives from the Jerusalem temple—the evening sacrifice. It is not night prayers, but prayer at a time of the day when work is over and one can rest and relax before eating and going to bed. Evening is a reflective time, a quiet period when one wants to thank God for the day, and praise him for what he is and for what he has done.

Compline is frankly night prayers, originally said "bedside" in the dormitory. With St. Benedict it never changes. It is short and had to be, with sleepy monks eyeing longingly their welcome beds.

Father Nathan Mitchell, in his article previously referred to, gives some statements from very early Christian writers about Christian prayer at these various times during the day and night. He concludes: "These few examples reveal that at an early age in the life of the Church, the scriptural principle of 'incessant prayer' was reinforced by the Christian custom of prayer (public and/or private) at definite times of day and night."[4]

The Hours of the *Opus Dei* consecrate time. No specific time of the day is without its period of common prayer. Night, dawn, sunrise, mid-morning, noon, the heat of the afternoon, sunset, and evening: each one is marked by the monks' coming together to praise the Creator. Again, this is something primitive and elemental, as all authentic religion should be, and akin to the four elements of antiquity and the Middle Ages: earth, air, water, fire. Benedictine spirituality is primitive in this sense of living with nature, and giving basic worship to the God of nature at natural times.

"Simple" might be a better word—living simply, and going to God who is simple, simply and directly. It is natural to Benedictines to want to consecrate the times of the day, as these times remind them of God and of their relation to him.

No matter what the work of the individual may be, no matter how sophisticated, the time of common prayer recalls to him that God is God and that he is only his very unnecessary creature; that over all and under all is God. Monks and nuns may be snatched from important work to praise God together, but there is nothing like an hour of the *Opus Dei* to bring home to them the fact that their work is not the *raison d' être* of their existence, and that work may change but the *Opus Dei* goes on.

The necessity of work has caused the most problems for the *Opus Dei* in modern times. Benedictines have traditionally had schools attached to their monasteries, but other types of work that are demanding and keep the community on a tight schedule also present similar problems. Before Vatican II a monastery might schedule Lauds, Prime, Terce, Sext, None and the Conventual Mass all before the community went to work at 8:30 A.M.! They would pick up the Office again around 5:00 P.M., but this left a work day without their coming together for common worship. In some houses Vespers, the prayer at sunset, was "covered" after lunch, and Matins (Vigils), the prayer of night, was said before the evening meal.

Monks of that era would refer to the *Opus Dei* as the *Onus Diei* (the burden of the day), but I think that they were well aware of the fact that the Office was supposed to be their first work. Facing a two-hour session of Office at five in the morning, particularly after a late night at a school function or a meeting, they came to realize that the reason for this was the fact that they were Benedictines and that their primary occupation was the praise of God in common.

What was lost was the association of the Hours of the Office with their proper time. And once their time-value was lost sight of, one of their purposes—to help the monk consecrate a particular time of the day or the night—was frustrated. Monks thought of "getting the Office in," rather than of interrupting their work to come together to praise God at natural sign posts of the day and renew their own consecration for the coming period.

Also lost sight of was the relation of the *Opus Dei* to continual prayer. A natural rhythm, an alternation of prayer and work, helped to keep the community in an atmosphere of prayer and aware of God's presence. A situation in which the Office was over by seven-thirty in the morning, and not resumed until five in the afternoon did not help.

All of this changed with Vatican II. The Constitution on the Sacred Liturgy, *Sacrosanctum Concilium*, stated: "Because the purpose of the Office is to sanctify the day, the traditional sequence of the Hours is to be restored so that once again they may be genuinely related to the time of the day when they are prayed, as far as this may be possible."[5] The result of the Constitution's legislation was an entirely new Divine Office. The traditional eight Hours were reduced to five: Matins (Vigils) became the Hour of Readings, Lauds became Morning Praise, Prime was suppressed, Terce, Sext, and None were compressed into a single day Hour, Vespers became Evening Praise, and Compline still served as night prayers. The entire psalter of 150 psalms, which was formerly recited each week, was now distributed over a four-week period, and the Office could now be recited in the vernacular.

The reason for the reduction of the number of psalms in the daily Office was this guiding principle: "Moreover, it will be necessary to take into account the modern conditions in which daily life has to be lived, especially by those who are called to labor in apostolic works."[6]

However, this new Office was arranged by the Church Fathers for the busy diocesan priests and those in the active religious Orders and Congregations. These were all bound to the Roman Divine Office, which had now been considerably shortened. It didn't really solve the problem for Benedictines who did not pray the Roman Office but rather one of their own—the Monastic Office, whose guidelines had been given by St. Benedict in his Rule.

In 1968 the Benedictines were permitted by the Sacred Congregation for Divine Worship:

1. to adopt the new Roman Divine Office;
2. to continue to pray their traditional Monastic Office or;
3. to allow each abbey and independent priory to arrange its own Office.

Guidelines for the third procedure were laid down at the meeting of all Benedictine abbots and independent priors in Rome in 1970. The bulk of the Office had to be, as heretofore, the psalms.

The result of this permission for plurality was, as can be guessed, complete plurality. Comparatively few monasteries retained the old Office, and the Latin. Others kept the Office but dropped the repetition of many psalms. Most monasteries adopted an Office that covered the psalter in two, three, or four week cycles. European monasteries were more apt to share Offices, whereas those in the United States preferred to do their own thing. However, the American abbeys based their distribution of the psalms on existing schemata that the abbots received from the Order's liturgical commission or on the Roman arrangement, while some made up their own.

After a period of experimentation, of shifting psalm distributions and translations, to say nothing of methods employed for scripture readings, things have quite settled down. What are the advantages of the new *Opus Dei*? For one thing it seems easier for monasteries that have schools or demanding businesses. With fewer psalms each week, rising can be later and more are able to be present for Lauds—if Lauds is the first hour of the day. Matins (or Hour of Readings) is also shorter, and more can attend before evening duties if the Hour is anticipated. Mass can now be offered at any time, so can be scheduled at a time when almost all of the community can attend. Hours of the Office are able to be combined with the community Mass, so if Mass is in the late morning, the Day Hour can precede it, or if before the evening meal, Vespers may be fit into it. Because there are fewer psalms, the whole effect is more restful, with the rat race phobia eliminated. Pauses during the Office have been restored, reminding the monks that the *Opus Dei* is prayer, and not mere recitation.

Another great advantage is the freedom to choose the readings for the Office. In the old Office there was not much variety in the short readings, or "Little Chapters" for Lauds, the Day Hours, and Vespers, and for Compline, none. Now whole books of the Bible can be read in small sections continuously. The first reading at Matins can be chosen on the same principle. The second reading should be from the Fathers and Doctors of the Church or from a Catholic "classic." Monasteries may and do take their Matins readings from those in the Roman Office.

With Prime eliminated and Terce, Sext, and None combined into one Day Hour, and with the implication that this latter Hour can now conveniently be recited during the workday, Benedictines no longer can have a day without coming together to praise God. Of course, this gathering is often for the community Mass, but when it isn't, the Day Hour provides the reason.

What are the disadvantages? After some years of the new Office the following stand out:

1. The full psalter that St. Benedict insisted upon is no longer recited each week;

2. the time spent on an Hour of the Office can be so short that the monks lose sight of the fact that they are doing the *Work* of God;

3. for the same reason, the Office can diminish in importance for the community, who come to lose respect for it as their first work;

4. the Roman Office permits the Hour of Readings to be said at any time, so if Benedictines adopt it, and schedule it as a daytime hour, it loses its significance as a prayer for the night, as a vigil service.

Can anything be done to eliminate these disadvantages? Should anything be done?

After arranging the Hours of the *Opus Dei* and determining their content, St. Benedict writes: "Above all else we urge that if anyone finds this distribution of the psalms unsatisfactory, he should arrange whatever he judges better, provided that the full complement of 150 psalms is by all means carefully maintained every week, and that the series begins anew each Sunday at Vigils. For monks who in a week's time say less than the full psalter with the customary canticles betray extreme indolence and lack of devotion in their service. We read, after all, that our holy Fathers, energetic as they were, did all this in a single day. Let us hope that we, lukewarm as we are, can achieve it in a whole week" (*RB 1980* 18, 22-25).

What Benedictines have to remember is that the completely revised Roman Divine Office, the Liturgy of the Hours, is intended for those who formerly prayed the old Roman Divine Office, as well as the laity who wish to use it, and that Benedictines did not pray this Office but their own Monastic Office. While, it is true, Benedictines belong to the Catholic Church also, and are able to adopt the Liturgy of the Hours, and even its principle of distributing the psalter throughout four weeks, they still have to face up to St. Benedict's principle for psalm distribution that I have just quoted. Benedictines are monks and nuns who are expected to pray more. Some may counter with "More is not necessarily better," but it is possible to retort that more can be a means to better for those who have only the one End.

A monastery that sees the *Opus Dei* as its first work is going to make it its first work. There has to be an element of work in the Office; monastics must make an effort to make it something worthwhile. It has to be worthy of what they are supposed to be doing. Benedictines have to respect their Office.

In this connection monks and nuns have to remember that the Office is the "sacrifice of praise"—that they are giving glory to the Father through, with, and in Christ who offered himself as a victim of glory, and still does through the community, who are victims with him. The *Opus Dei* can never be a token service, painless and convenient. In a busy day "something's got to give," but it shouldn't always be the *Opus Dei*.

Seventy years ago Dom Germain Morin wrote, "If ever, which God forbid, the liturgical chant should come to be neglected among us—if the long hours passed in Choir should be changed, little by little, into an exercise purely material and unaesthetic—that moment would give the deathblow to enthusiasm for Divine worship—that enthusiasm without which, as we have said, there can be no true monks."[7]

One important aspect of the *Opus Dei* that has developed through the centuries is that of the Divine Office as the prayer of the Church.

What began with St. Benedict as the common prayer of the monastery is today part of the Liturgy of the Church and its official prayer. Benedictines have the obligation and privilege of praying as the Church and for the Church. This is not in any way a radical departure from St. Benedict's concept, but simply a greatly enriching development.

Even in St. Benedict's time, and through the centuries before the Divine Office was considered to be part of the Liturgy and the official prayer of the Church, the Benedictine community which gathered to pray the *Opus Dei* was praying as and for the Church. Long before monks had the obligation to pray the Office because they were in holy orders and professed solemn vows, they regarded their simple community Office as reaching out beyond their own numbers and the walls of the monastery to embrace and include all the Church—militant, suffering, and triumphant. The *Opus Dei* was truly ecclesial, not just local.

This point leads naturally into my last topic in this chapter, how to pray the *Opus Dei*. We turn first to the Holy Rule to read St. Benedict's terse instructions in Chapter 19. "We believe that the divine presence is everywhere. . . . But beyond the least doubt we should believe this to be especially true when we celebrate the Divine Office." Here is his basic principle: the Benedictine stands before God. "Let us consider, then, how we ought to behave in the presence of God and his angels, and let us stand to sing the psalms in such a way that our minds are in harmony with our voices." Such instruction needs no commentary, only amplification.

When monks and nuns pray the Divine Office they are joining the angels in the direct worship of God. Over and above every other consideration, praying for personal and local needs, or even for the universal Church, their main reason for this activity is to give God glory—the glory of adoration, praise, love, and thanksgiving. The Office is totally God-centered. What the monastics are saying throughout is "Thou!" The choir becomes heaven, where the members are anticipating what they hope to be doing eternally—giving glory to the Father, and the Son, and the Holy Spirit.

Although the *Opus Dei* is community prayer, its value derives from the fact that it is basically the personal prayer of each member. It has to be the worship that comes from the adoring heart of each one. How can it be the community's worship if each person who makes up the community is not giving God all the worship that he can? Psalms that may not be meaningful to the individual become so when they are seen as fuel for giving glory. Monastics have to remember what the *Opus Dei* is—the common prayer of a group of cenobites, each one of whom is seeking God with his whole heart. Therefore mind and will must be in harmony with the voice.

Personal prayer it is, but not bounded by the purely personal, because its object is Someone infinitely greater than the person. Then, too, the monk or nun stands as part of a whole which, in turn, is part of the Body of Christ in the Whole Christ. In Christ, the Head of this Body, he or she is taken into the community of the Trinity.

The community at prayer is the Church at prayer. This is a great incentive to prayer for the individual. Psalms take on entirely different meanings when one realizes that he is the Church behind the Iron Curtain and in other parts of the world where the Church is hampered and persecuted; that he embodies in himself the poor, the ill, the dying, the depressed, lonely and despairing people. The narrow bounds of his choir stall expand to take in everybody. Praying an hour of the Divine Office as the Church and for the Church can be a self-shattering experience.

The Divine Office is part of the Liturgy of the Church—its official prayer. While the monk may center upon the *official* aspect of the Liturgy, he can neglect its most important, its fundamental element: in the Liturgy, Christ, the perfect priest, gives the Father the perfect worship of his human nature for the human race with whom he has become one.[8]

What a great dimension the *Opus Dei* takes on when seen as Christ giving the Father glory through the prayer of the monks and nuns! Here is an endless topic for meditation. Not only is Christ praying this particular hour of the Office through them, but they are glorifying the Father through Christ and with him, because they are in him.

Then when we consider the Liturgical Year, we become aware that Christ's earthly life is made present each year as in a time machine, and that he is still giving the Father the glory *now* that he gave him *then* in all the actions, sufferings, and conditions of his earthly life. Again, how different the psalms become when we realize that it is Christ praying them. He did pray them then; he knew them by heart, as every good Jew did. He prayed from the psalms as he hung on the Cross. The Benedictine must have the mind of Christ when He prayed the psalms, and let Him continue this way of glorifying His Father through him. Just a week of praying the psalms as Christ will reveal to the monk or nun those references to His death and resurrection that He pointed out to the disciples (Lk. 24:27, 44).

The *Opus Dei* is meant to be the focal point of the monastic day. Nothing is to be preferred to it (*RB*, ch. 43). If a novice has an authentic monastic vocation, he has to have a great desire for it (*RB*, ch. 58). It is *the* Work for God. Individually and collectively, Benedictines have to make it worthy of what it is.

NOTES

[1]Note that St. Benedict calls the *Opus Dei* the *divine office* in Chapter 43, which means literally the *divine duty*. The *Opus Dei* is usually called the Divine Office, which term designates the official and liturgical prayer of the Church.

[2]Cf. Nathan Mitchell, OSB, "The Liturgical Code in the Rule of Benedict," in *RB 1980,* pp. 379-414. The *Rule of the Master* was probably a source for St. Benedict in writing his Rule. Cf. Luke Eberle, OSB, ed., *The Rule of the Master* (Kalamazoo: Cistercian Publications, 1977).

[3]Cf. Mitchell, *loc. cit.,* pp. 380-382.

[4]*Ibid.,* p. 381.

[5]Ch. 4, no. 88, in *The Sixteen Documents of Vatican II* (Boston: St. Paul Editions, n. d.), p. 42.

[6]*Ibid.*

[7]*The Ideal of the Monastic Life Found in the Apostolic Age* (Westminster, MD: The Newman Press, 1950), pp. 117-118.

[8]Cf. *Constitution on the Sacred Liturgy,* Ch. 4, no. 83, in *op. cit.,* pp. 40-41.

VI

The Benedictine Way

THE BENEDICTINE WAY, considered as the road that monks and nuns take in the pursuit of God, is actually a series of steps going up to the level of union with God. St. Benedict describes twelve steps, or rungs of a ladder, but the level is certainly reached by the seventh step.[1] There is no other way for the Benedictine in the search for God.

The novice begins on the first step and may be professed before reaching the sixth. The rapidity of the climb depends on the individual and on God. The steps of humility are not a thirty-day exercise. A certain leisure is demanded, rather an unconcern with time, so that the novice or monk can devote himself to God.

The ascent may be comparatively steady or it may take years. When the person reaches union with God it is possible that he may slip back into his old love affair with Self, and have to start the climb again with Step One. I think that we grizzled veterans will have to admit that monks are usually somewhere on the steps of humility. St. Benedict conceives of the whole process of the spiritual life as a growth in humility. I will not comment on that fact now, because his thought will become apparent as we study each step.[2]

"The first step of humility, then, is that a man keeps the fear of God always before his eyes (Ps. 36:2) and never forgets it. He must constantly remember everything God has commanded, keeping in mind that all who despise God will burn in hell for their sins, and all who fear God have everlasting life awaiting them. While he guards himself at every moment from sins or vices of thought or tongue, of hand or foot, of self-will or bodily desire, let him recall that he is always seen by God in heaven, that his actions everywhere are in God's sight and are reported by angels at every hour" (*RB 1980* 7, 10-13).[3]

The first step of humility, then, is the fear of God. This comprises the Benedictine's basic attitude toward God; it is the foundation of the life of seeking God and enjoying union with him—it is the individual's rock-bottom disposition. The monk does not think of God as a "pal," a "chum," for he knows who God is and who he himself is.

St. Benedict demands this disposition elsewhere in the Rule. The Abbot should do all things in the fear of God (ch. 3); the monk obeys at once "in the speed of the fear of God" (ch. 5); the procurator must be a person who fears God (ch. 31), so must the infirmarian (ch. 36), the guest-master (ch. 53), and the porter (ch. 66). He closes his Rule desiring that his monks fear God and prefer nothing whatever to Christ (ch. 72).

St. Benedict's fear of God is the same as biblical fear of God, which expresses man's "whole religious relationship."[4] It is simply the attitude that a person should have with regard to God—his basic attitude in life. What he habitually thinks about God, and therefore about his relationship with God, serves as the foundation for his other attitudes and includes such aspects as obedience, love, willingness to listen to God's word in his life, and a deep sense of the transcendence of God.

What St. Benedict wants the monk to grasp on the first step is the *difference* between God and himself, the infinite gap. When he deeply realizes this, then he can understand God's rights over him, his duties toward God, and the fact of reward and punishment.

We can summarize the monk's activity on the first step by four questions which he should answer:

1. Who is God?
2. Who am I?
3. What is the relationship between this God and this I?
4. What are the consequences?

In answering the first question, the novice will find it helpful to search for the answer in the Bible. He should learn the biblical attributes of God. There he will follow God's own revelation of himself.

One attribute that stands out in the Old Testament is God's holiness. The Hebrew word that *holiness* translates, *Qodesh,* has as its root meaning *separate.* So when the Bible says that God is holy it means that he is separate, entirely separate from his creation.

How is God separate? God is the Source of existence, of being, he is the Giver, and creation is the given (and the given to). He is the one who alone loves with "steadfast love." He alone is the End of creation whose purpose is to give him glory.[5]

Holiness is the biblical way of referring to the *divine nature*, that which makes God to be God. "The Wholly Other" is Rudolf Otto's felicitous translation.

The answers to the other questions are in the Bible also. However, that to "Who am I?" is not readily apparent.

The Bible sees man as being flesh, soul, and spirit. Flesh is the person related to material creation, to animals, minerals, plants—to the whole human race. It is his horizontal dimension. When the Word became flesh, God the Son took on a kinship to matter in all its orders.

Soul means man as living, alive, but it also denotes the human person, the responsible agent of his own action. Soul presumes a being who can think, will, choose, who can obey and disobey—self-determine.

Spirit is this flesh-soul being but oriented to union with God. Spirit is the person's vertical dimension, that in him which makes him want to go "up, up, and away." Spirit takes him out of himself to search for Truth, Good, Beauty. Man loves because he is spirit.

Biblical man experiences a polarity, a twofold attraction: he is pulled between heaven and earth. In the middle of these two intersecting dimensions stands the person, who must decide. The perfect biblical man does not opt for one dimension to the exclusion of the other, but achieves a balance in which spirit guides soul, and both rule flesh.

The novice on the first step of humility must reckon with these three aspects before he can objectively answer the question, Who am I? If he doesn't, he may end up counting his assets and accomplishments and miss St. Benedict's whole point. What St. Benedict wants is for him to see who he is in contrast with God—a creature, endowed by his Creator with existence, with an intellect and will that can know and choose Truth and Good, as God can, and having a capacity for God. *Endowed* by his Creator, because all that he is by creation is pure gift, without God he would not be, and without God's continual gift he would be annihilated.

St. Benedict wants him to face up to the fact of what he has done with God's gift, what *he* has made of himself as flesh-soul-spirit. He has to face the sorry fact of himself—sensual, selfish, self-centered—the great capacity for God that he has filled instead with things and self. He has frustrated himself as the image of God.

He has to face God. To become a monk there is no other way. This is truly the first step for him in his monastic life. He has to be like Moses realizing the presence of God in the burning bush—"And Moses hid his face, for he was afraid to look at God" (Ex. 3:6). Conversion begins when a person meets God, and the monastic life is a conversion. Only this confrontation with God will make a person see the infinite gap between God and himself and leave him prone on his face in adoration and contrition.

This realization of God is actually a grace, a mystical grace. The novice can and should do what he can to impress upon himself God's transcendence and his other attributes, but in the long run the really shattering experience of God that I have spoken of has to be by God's gift. It has to be such as will affect one's whole life. Only God can give such a grace.

From this encounter the novice and the professed monk realize their obligations toward God and the consequences. The fear of God results in a great fidelity to God's will. Sin is choosing self instead of God. But when a person fully grasps the unbounded transcendence of God, he is going to choose God instead of self. His own will he sees now as being somehow allied with God's. He is also beginning to understand what loving God means.

We notice in what St. Benedict says about the first step that he really says nothing much about loving God. He will treat of love when he speaks about the second and third steps. But true, solid love of God has to be founded on the person's recognition of the difference between God and himself. If we can only love a person for his superior goods, we can only love God when we know him as infinite good.

So, to sum up this first step of humility, we see that, where other spiritualities may begin with the lovableness of various aspects of Christ's humanity, the Benedictine way begins with the tremendous awesomeness of God. It sees through the humanity of Christ to his divine nature and Person, that of God the Son who was eternally with the Father and the Spirit one God before he took a human nature.

In today's secular humanistic culture, many men and women enter the priesthood and religious life to serve mankind. The Benedictine applicant may come to serve his fellow man, but then the novice master helps him up to the first step of humility where, naked and alone, he has to face God. He comes to see that God is all: the Source and End of all creation. When the novice firmly grasps this fact, he can then serve mankind because he loves in people what God loves—God himself. He looks for God in others, but he cannot effectively do this until he has met God on this First Step. Like the prophets, like his father St. Benedict, the monk has to be truly a man of God—*vir Dei*—as St. Gregory called St. Benedict.

"The second step of humility is that a person, loving not his own will, delight not in carrying out his desires, but imitates by his actions that word of the Lord, 'I came not to do my own will but the will of him who sent me' (Jn. 6:38). Again the Scripture says, 'Self-will merits punishment, but self-constraint wins a crown' " (*RB* 7, 31-33). There is a great amount of Christian theology packed into these few words, but we are only able here to delineate the leading ideas.

First, the novice on the second step faces the fact of Christ. "What do you think of the Christ? Whose son is he?" (Mt. 22:42). He realizes that he is the Son of God and the Son of man, that is God and Man. He meditates on the reason why God the Son, in a point of time, became one with the human race: "I came that they may have life, and have it abundantly" (Jn. 10:10). He gave this life, his own life with the Father, when he gave his Spirit at his death (cf. Jn. 19:30; also 20:22).

But he had to merit this life for the human race. Adam had this life originally but lost it by his disobedience; he also lost it for his descendants. A second Adam had to come to gain it back. How would he be able to do this? By his obedience. Only the perfect obedience of the God-Man could atone for mankind's self-will and self-centered desires, and merit for it the life of God. Christ's obedience we know was "unto death, even death on a cross" (Phil. 2:8). So really Christ came to obey so "that they may have life."

In the Trinity the Son's role is to love the Father. The Son-become-man's role is to obey him because for Christ (and for us) obedience is love. How conscious he was of this role while he was visible on earth!

How many times he referred to "him who sent me"! He knew that every move, every omission, was dictated by the Father's will. He obeyed not only as himself but as the whole human race.

All of this the novice comes to realize as he looks at the crucifix. He comes to understand not the "folly of the Cross," but the folly of self-will and selfish desires that frustrate the person, who is made for union with God and for living by His life.

On the first step the novice learned that sin opposes God's will because it opposes God; because it is the creature choosing self instead of God. On the second step the novice sees the utter injustice to God of such a choice, that there is an offense to God by the very nature of the wrong choice, and that this wrong choice has to be repaired. He learns this by learning about Christ.

Then, too, he sees Christ taking on himself the most painful task of making this reparation and it suddenly dawns on him that Christ did this for him. He exclaims, with a burst of love, he "loved me and gave himself for me!" (Gal. 2:20). Love attracts love, and that is what happens on the second step. The novice loves not his own will because he is coming to love Christ.

He loves Christ and imitates what He does, not his own will but the will of the Father who sent Him. He obeys Christ's commands and even his counsels: "If a man loves me, he will keep my word . . . and the word which you hear is not mine but the Father's who sent me" (Jn. 14:23-24). In short, the person on the second step sincerely desires to do God's will because he sees God as his only true love object. The question for him is: How can I always be certain that I am doing God's will?

"The third degree of humility is that a person for love of God submit himself to a superior in obedience, imitating the Lord, of whom the Apostle says, 'He became obedient unto death' " (Phil. 2:8) (*RB 1980* 7, 34).

This submission goes back to the Desert Fathers. How many times we read that a younger monk will come to the cell of a veteran monk with the request, "Father, give me a word to live by." The younger needs a guide, a truly charismatic leader, who knows how to live a life of seeking God. There is no legal bond here, no vow, but simply handing on the teaching of the Bible and the traditions of the Desert—in short, wisdom, a word to live by. Many old abbas took in disciples who were there to learn. The obedience of the latter was that of apprentices, absorbing the know-how of their masters.

So the charismatic leader of a Benedictine monastery has to have this know-how and the example that proves to his disciples that he truly knows how to live (cf. *RB*, chs. 2 and 64). He has to be "learned in the Divine Law," a person whose *lectio divina* overflows to the community with "new things and old" (ch. 64).

St. Benedict in his Rule has codified the teaching of the Bible and the Desert tradition on the life of seeking God in close union with others, and he leaves it to his followers as a minimal rule for beginners (ch. 73). He leaves it particularly to abbots to be not only their guide but also their standard. A Benedictine abbot is to rule by the Holy Rule. Because the Jerusalem Church regarded St. Peter as the vicar of Christ, so does the existential church of a Benedictine monastery regard the abbot or abbess as holding the place of Christ. While this may seem to place a burden on the community, it is only a burden of faith which, thank God, is infused; the real burden is on the abbot to let Christ live.

On the third step the novice makes his decision to be a monk. Of course he more or less made it before he entered the monastery, but on this step he makes a deep commitment to follow Christ alone. He makes the decision to obey God the Father speaking through his Son to the abbot. He does this out of love of God. On the first step he learned the "God-ness" of God; on the second, the infinite loveableness of God. Now he decides to return love for love. There is no fear here, no necessity. His decision does not come out of his desire to save his soul. He does not decide to obey because he wants to join the monks in the kind of work they do. The decision of the third step is motivated purely by love of God. If the novice does not have this motive, he is in for trouble. There is no by-passing or skipping this step.

"The fourth step of humility is that if in this obedience he has to suffer because of difficult or contrary things, or even unjust injuries, he embrace patience with a quiet mind, and, persevering, grow not weary nor depart, for Scripture says, 'He who endures to the end will be saved' (Mt. 10:22), and 'Let your heart take courage and wait for the Lord' (Ps. 27:14)" (*RB* 7, 35-37).

The novice has already experienced some of the difficulties that St. Benedict sets forth as characteristic of this step. The older Benedictine, climbing again the twelve steps as a kind of "refresher course," knows them only too well from his own experience. The whole idea of this step is that the monk should persevere in his obedience no matter what happens, because he knows that by means of obedience he receives God's will with regard to himself. In wanting to be sure about God's will, he submits his will to that of a man of God, a man of the Spirit, who is himself committed to living by the Rule of St. Benedict and is approved of and blessed by the Church to lead others to God by this Rule. He is seeking God, and the most fundamental place to find Him is in His will.

The novice, in wanting God's will, wants God. In obeying that will he is loving God. Christ gave the Father the glory of love by carrying out the work that the Father gave him to do (Jn. 17:4). So, to obey out of love is actually love, love in "Spirit and in truth."

This love, in order to be true, has to be tested. In this time of trial God wills difficult things, tasks and conditions that go against everything that the novice wants for himself. These are crucifying to his pride, his sensuality, and his desire to possess. Obedience will strip him of everything that is not God. Of course God doesn't need to test him for his own sake. God knows. But the novice has to know himself, his strengths and weaknesses, and know whether he is truly seeking God. His superiors have to know, and so do his brethren who will vote on him.

True love will only grow and develop by means of trials. It has to emerge unscathed, whole and entire, pure and unalloyed, from all the tests to which God submits it. This is the only way that love can exist as true love, the love that has been tried by fire.

The fourth step is a time of asceticism, a time to exercise the virtues—what the ancients called the "active life." The novice now discovers the necessity of holding on to love of God by means of faith, hope, fortitude, temperance, prudence, and justice, to say nothing of love of neighbor. (I daresay that now he is really learning to love his neighbor as Christ. He begins to see that he is living with human beings and a variety of characters, as St. Benedict foresaw every community would be.)

We must not think of the obedience of the fourth step as being task obedience. Sometimes Benedictines see it only as such—hanging on to obedience when the abbot gives one a very difficult assignment. What St. Benedict is thinking about here are the difficulties and contrary things that the person will experience because he is a Christian. The monastic life is nothing else but a perfecting of the Christian life. The abbot or abbess takes Christ's place in this particular segment of the Church. What he or she has to say to the community is what Christ wants to say to *these* Christians. After all, the Rule of St. Benedict is not a manual for whipping into shape the staff of an institution, but a guide for the school of the Lord's service.

A Benedictine may find his work enjoyable and stimulating, but have great problems with the teaching of Christ: he can chafe under the yoke of his vows; he may even find his ambition and talents confined in what he considers a "menial task." The obedience that the individual is called on to give is the gift of his whole self to God for his whole life; to do out of love, and as love, God's whole will for him. Of course he is going to suffer in the doing, but true love perseveres.

After giving the essence of the fourth step, St. Benedict urges the monk to persevere in obedience by presenting a number of biblical passages. These all refer to perseverance in the life of union with God or the Christian life in general. They do not refer to accepting and carrying out an assignment, nor does St. Benedict point them in that direction. I think that St. Benedict's most helpful advice to the monk who is having his troubles with obedience is this: "he should embrace patience with a silent mind." This can be expanded to: You will suffer better if you don't think about what's causing the suffering. The more conscious we are of our pain the more it hurts.

His next most helpful advice is what he says at the end of the third step: "imitating the Lord, of whom the Apostle says, 'He became obedient unto death' " (Phil. 2:8). If the monk can fill his silent mind with the sufferings of Christ, think about the reason for these sufferings, his own place in them, and suffer with and as Christ, he will have "clear sailing"—not painless, but clear.

This fourth step is going to take a little time. It includes what the medieval spiritual writers called the purgative and the illuminative ways. On this step the Benedictine is learning Christ by experience, as a Divine Person and as human. It is an affective time in his life. He is drawn to and warmed by Christ's human side. His prayer is affective: it is all praise, thanks, love, contrition, petition.

The novice is also deeply learning himself by his ups and particularly by his downs. As he learns Christ, he learns that he is a huge contrast to Christ. When Christ shows him the Father he is as prostrate on the ground as the apostles were on Mount Tabor. And when the Father reveals Christ as the Son, he wants to sink into the earth. As a result, he has a great desire to confess his unworthiness.

"The fifth step of humility is that a monk does not hide from the abbot all the evil thoughts that come into his heart, nor his hidden sins, but manifests them in humble confession" (*RB* 7, 44). St. Benedict does not mean sacramental confession here but the manifestation of one's state of soul to his spiritual father. This was the custom of the Desert: as one depended on one's abba for guidance to purity of heart, so the abba depended on the monk's complete openness with him so that he might know what word to give.

In St. Benedict's monastery, the abbot is by his office the spiritual father. On his climb up the steps of humility the novice has acquainted the abbot with his problems. Up to now he has always found these manifestations difficult to make, and more often than not has not told the abbot everything. He has been afraid lest the abbot lose his good impression of him (which the novice presumes that the abbot has). But as a result of the fourth step a change takes place: the novice wants to tell the abbot everything. What has happened? The Holy Spirit is beginning to take over his life.

On the fourth step the novice realized his great sinfulness from his struggles with simple Christianity and from his falls. He learned a side of himself that he never faced before: his bad side, the deep causes of his falls and struggles. He had to face those moments of truth when it dawned on him that he is not the nice guy he always thought he was.

Outside the monastery he could have killed the pain with a couple of drinks. Here he has to live conscious of the truth about himself. Now, on the fifth step, he feels that he really needs help, and he is happy to "tell all" to his spiritual father. We can clearly see God's grace in all of this. God has to show the person what he is not, in contrast with Himself, before the person can see God at all.

I cannot stress too much the need for a guide up the steps of humility. In fact, it is one of the marks of a Benedictine to realize this necessity and to find one. As he learns from his abba the ways of God and the ways of himself he can eventually walk by the sole guidance of the Holy Spirit. A good spiritual father will look to the day when he can cut the spiritual umbilical cord, but not too soon. The monk will never reach the state when he can entirely dispense with the help of his abba.

Do today's Benedictines have to make the abbot their spiritual director in order to be true to the fifth step? No, because since St. Benedict penned those lines, choir monks have gone on to Holy Orders. Having a number of priest-monks available gives the Benedictine a choice of confessors, and it is a good thing for one's confessor to be one's spiritual director because he should, to be an effective minister of reconciliation, know the whole person and his problems. Of course, by grace of state, the abbot is *the* spiritual father, and monks should be willingly open with him and rely on him for direction within the community.

The search for a spiritual father is not always easy. What the monk is looking for is a wise man who, as I said, knows the ways of God and the ways of the monk. The latter must not stop with one who makes him feel comfortable, but must find one who can strip away, layer by layer, the monk's Self so he will know what God wants to do with him. He needs to know how to reach God.

"The sixth step of humility is that a monk is content with the lowest and most menial treatment, and regards himself as a poor and worthless workman in whatever task he is given, saying to himself with the Prophet: 'I am insignificant and ignorant, no better than a beast before you, yet I am with you always' (Ps. 73:22-23)" (*RB 1980* 7, 49-50).

The clue to the meaning of the sixth step is in the passage from Psalm 73. What has happened is that the novice has become a contemplative. When did this happen? Probably before he left the fourth step.

The contemplative state is that in which God's action is more preponderant in a person's life than his own. How can a person be content "with the lowest and most menial treatment" except by grace? He can reason out, coldly and objectively, that he is "a poor and worthless workman" in some jobs that are given to him. No great grace is necessary for that, only sad experience. Impractical people are no good at changing tires or even at putting up storm windows, but tell them they're no good at playing the piano when they have a conservatory certificate! Yet they have to regard themselves as poor and worthless pianists? It can't be done naturally and rationally. It can only be done by way of contrast with God—"no better than a beast before you." In other words, by *God's* action.

Once a person realizes who God is and loves him because of his infinite worth, he and his accomplishments don't seem like much. From the vantage point of God he knows that all that he is and has is by courtesy of God. But to enjoy the vantage point of God he has to be brought there by God. It is a gift, a grace. "Yet I am always with you!"

When a person reaches the contemplative state he lives by the Gifts of the Holy Spirit. These are, we know, seven kinds of ability that are given in baptism that enable the person to receive corresponding power and inspirations from the Holy Spirit. John of St. Thomas (d. 1644) compares them to seven sails on a boat, capable of receiving the powerful "wind" of the Holy Spirit. He compares the seven virtues to oars: although the rower has the advantage of the leverage of the oarlocks, the work of rowing is still up to him. But when a favorable wind blows, he can put up his oars and let the wind do the work.[6]

So the novice on the sixth step is acting by the Gifts of Fear of God, Knowledge, Understanding, and Wisdom. Four kinds of powerful God-given inspirations enable him to realize who it is whom he is always with, and who he is in contrast with God—"no better than a beast."

Is it possible to be on the sixth step and not be a contemplative? Yes, but it may be more rare than we think. If a person can be contented with the worst treatment and judge himself to be a poor and worthless workman just by adding up reasons presented by his intellect alone, he can be a noncontemplative sixth-stepper. But to do this he still needs the help of grace, and powerful grace at that.

He needs to really be *convinced* he needs some good gusts of the Gifts. He may not be aware of their operation, he may not *feel* them, but the proof is in their results. It's one thing to have an academic knowledge of one's worthlessness in contrast with God and of the justice of unjust treatment, and quite another to be content with the situation as a *fait accompli*, to be *convinced* of the justice. The intellect can reason but only the Spirit can convince.

The Gifts of the Holy Spirit can be operative daily. Father Reginald Garrigou-Lagrange, O.P. defended the thesis that infused contemplation is the normal development of the virtues of Faith, Hope, and especially Charity, and of the Gifts of the Holy Spirit, all infused into the soul at baptism. Since 1923, when his book[7] appeared, theologians have come to the conclusion that the Gifts are not for the great moments in life only but for the daily crises as well.

Theologians and mystics tell us that the Holy Spirit gives his power by way of the Gifts to those who are sincerely working at purity of heart, to those who are truly seeking God. This is what the novice has been doing all along, ever since he has been on the first step. Moreover, he has been attempting to pray always, to have more protracted periods of prayer—for *lectio divina* and other forms of private prayer. He gives God the worship of praise in the *Opus Dei*, and offers to the Father the glory of Christ's sacrifice in the Mass. He should at this stage be in some sort of condition to hope that the Holy Spirit will take him over. Until he does, he has to *want* to be content with the worst, and *want* to judge himself as a pretty useless character. And he should pray fervently but patiently for the Spirit's action. "Let your heart take courage and wait for the Lord!" (Ps. 27).

"The seventh step of humility is that a man not only admits with his tongue but is also convinced in his heart that he is inferior to all and of less value" (*RB 1980* 7, 51).

This step is actually the top step of the staircase of humility, the remaining five steps are only the results of the seventh, and external manifestations of the interior that God has given the novice on that step.[8] And God-given it is. To be convinced in the depth of one's heart that he is inferior to all, and the cheapest in price, supposes God's action. This step definitely places the person in the contemplative state.

What has grown at this stage is the novice's love of God. His obedience has become love, developed and deepened, because tested by adversities in which he has persevered, aided by the infused virtues—his oars. The Gifts have brought him safely home.

Loving God by God's own love, the Holy Spirit, he necessarily is now able to regard himself as the last and least of the whole human race. But he can rejoice in this because now he wants only God.

There is one more degree of love that St. Benedict gives: "Now, therefore, after ascending all these steps of humility, the monk will quickly arrive at that perfect love of God which casts out fear (1 Jn. 4:18). Through this love, all that he once performed with dread, he will now begin to observe without effort, as though naturally, from habit, no longer out of fear of hell, but out of love for Christ, good habit and delight in virtue. All this the Lord will by the Holy Spirit graciously manifest in his workman now cleansed of vices and sins" (*RB 1980* 7, 67-70).

We see, then, what St. Benedict has been doing all along. What seemed like the steps of humility have been actually the steps of the love of God. And the agent in all of this has been the Holy Spirit!

I think that this top degree of love is what Walter Hilton describes in *The Scale of Perfection.* He says, "But perfect humility comes when the intellect is illumined to see God. For when the Holy Ghost illumines the reason to see the truth, how God is all and does all, the soul is so carried away by love and joy that it becomes oblivious of itself, and gives itself to the contemplation of God with all the love of which it is capable."[9]

It isn't that the person makes a formal judgment of himself as the least and last of all, as that he takes the fact for granted when he finally realizes God. Actually he ignores himself.

"But the lover of God has this humility continually, without difficulty and without effort, but rather with pleasure and joy...because his mind is illumined to know the truth and the excellence of God through the gift of the Holy Ghost."[10]

"He had rather...think only of God and get humility in that way. And that is much the safest way for whoever can attain it."[11] And that, I presume to add, is the Benedictine way.

NOTES

[1]St. Benedict envisions a *scala,* which can mean a ladder or a staircase. Although *RB 1980* translates it as the former, in 7:6, 8-9, it translates *gradus* as step. I think that for practical purposes it is easier to picture the monk on a staircase rather than on a ladder.

[2]This is the approach of John Nicholas Grou, S.J. in his *Spiritual Maxims,* (Springfield, IL: Templegate, 1961), pp. 1-13. Pere Grou died in 1803, and his book has become a classic.

[3]St. Benedict then develops what I have given here as the essence of the first step by a number of biblical passages (*RB* 7, 14-30).

[4]Walther Eichrodt, *Theology of the Old Testament* (Philadelphia: Westminster Press, 1967), vol. II, p. 268. Cf. pp. 268-277.

[5]Read, e.g., Is. 40, 41, 43; Mt. 5:43-48.

[6]John of St. Thomas, *The Gifts of the Holy Ghost* (London: Sheed and Ward, 1951), pp. 56-57.

[7]English translation, *Christian Perfection and Contemplation* (St. Louis: B. Herder Book Co., 1939).

[8]The remaining steps are: 8th, to follow the example of the seniors; 9th, to be silent until questioned; 10th, not to be ready to laugh; 11th, when one speaks, to do so simply and humbly; 12th, to let one's humility be manifest to others by one's exterior.

[9]Dom Gerard Sitwell, OSB, translator and editor (Westminster, MD: Newman Press, 1953), p. 261. This is in Book II, ch. 37.

[10]*Ibid.,* pp. 262-263.

[11]*Ibid.,* p. 263.

VII
Urbs Jerusalem Beata!

THE SPECIFICALLY BENEDICTINE VOWS that monks and nuns make, while made to God, are certainly conditioned by the monastery in which they live. These are *conversatio morum,* stability, and obedience, and they can in reality be reduced to one, for what the new monk or nun promises is simply that he or she will henceforth live the monastic way of life as lived in *this* monastery and interpreted by *this* abbot or abbess.

The vow *conversatio morum* means the monastic life according to the Rule of St. Benedict. The reason why I present it in the original Latin is that for almost twelve hundred years Benedictines have been professing something else—*conversio morum*—which means the conversion of one's morals or manners.

St. Benedict says that the monk who is making his profession promises stability, *conversatione morum suorum,* and obedience. Some two hundred years after St. Benedict it was difficult to understand just what he meant by this expression, so copyists changed it to *conversione morum suorum.* In recent times critical editions of the Rule have restored the original to the text, beginning with that of Abbot Butler in 1912, and scholars have debated its meaning ever since.[1]

Conversatio means manner of life, habitual way of acting, conduct, but *conversatio morum suorum* is either clumsy or meaningless—the manner of life of one's morals! No wonder it was changed to *conversion of manners.* But in 1959 Dom Basil Steidle of Beuron gave a satisfactory solution to the problem: the puzzling term was a low Latin idiom of St. Benedict's time, a "genitive of identity," and it meant *his manner of life and moral conduct,* or *his manner of life, that is, his moral conduct.*[2]

RB 1980 translates the term as *fidelity to monastic life* (58, 17). In 1937 Dom Justin McCann concluded that it should be translated simply as *self-discipline*. But he had to admit that St. Benedict meant "the special monastic discipline."[3]

Conversion of morals, or *reformation of life*, what's the difference? Actually there is no difference. The novice promises, as novices have promised for almost twelve centuries, that he will daily reform his life, and work at perfection according to the Rule of St. Benedict, not just a life of perfection in general. It is a very definite kind of life. This was the vow professed by so many Benedictine saints and countless other holy monks and nuns who reached holiness because they lived the monastic life and were model Benedictines. It is the Benedictine way.

He promises that he will pursue only one end—union with God—and that he will seek Him in His will. He promises that he will also seek Him in much *lectio divina*, go to Him in continual prayer, join his brothers in the prayer of the Church, and Christ in His sacrifice of glory to the Father. He willingly accepts the fact that his monastery is the immediate Church for him.

The vow of *conversatio* means that the Holy Rule is going to be a manual for the monk, a working document, a book that provides words to live by for his way of life, not a museum piece that serves merely to give a link with a long tradition.

I said at the beginning of this chapter that the novice vows the monastic way of life as lived in *this* monastery. This is the only condition in which the monastic life exists. It does not exist in the Rule of St. Benedict. The newcomer, as well as the critical old-timer, has to realize this postulate well. The Rule describes and legislates for the Benedictine life, but this doesn't become a reality until some people live it somewhere. It is a truly existential thing. As seen in the Rule the monastic life is ideal and theoretical, just as the anatomy and physiology of the human body are ideal and theoretical as they are presented in a textbook. Apart from a monastery there is no Benedictine monastic life.

It's up to a group of men or women to make the Holy Rule work. And that brings us to the vow of stability. By this vow the novice joins one of these groups. The bond is like that of marriage, "until death do us part," and "for better or for worse." (Father Choleric in a recent homily to our community said that there are times when a monk feels like singing that old song, "I Picked a Lemon in the Garden of Love.")

It is the vow of stability, binding this particular group together, that makes up a monastery. It is a very necessary vow because it just doesn't attach a person to a monastery, it makes him a vital part of a living and working group. During the formation period the solemnly professed observe the junior, and when he comes up to the vote before his solemn profession they decide whether they want him in. Meanwhile he has been observing them and decides whether he wants to be one of them. Because, after all, a person doesn't join a place or a work but a group of people who live in that place and who do the work.

The vow of stability doesn't attach one to a place but to a localized community. The community can move to a different place, but because a community usually doesn't, the monk becomes attached to the place, and should. It is his home, and he should love it, and even become at least mildly acquainted with all its trees. But he must always remember that his vow is to people. I say this because monastics can get like cats and become place-oriented.

The vow of stability has a great influence on the monastic observance. If it's this vow that gets this group together, and the monastic life is this group actually living it, then I would say, it is this vow that makes the monastic life possible. So when a person makes the vow of stability he or she is promising to cooperate with a definite group in living the monastic life. It brings the vow of *conversatio* down to a concrete situation.

The three Benedictine vows narrow down in focus: *conversatio* is to a life, stability is to a group, and obedience is to a person.

The abbot or abbess directs the life of the Rule. I will not repeat what has already been said about the abbot in the last chapter, but one point must be stressed here: the relation of the abbot to the group in interpreting the Rule and in executing its prescriptions.

The Benedictine vow of obedience is not to community consensus, nor to a General Chapter, but to one person: the abbot or abbess. True, the Church gives the community certain rights and power of decision in its official chapter meetings, but the superior's role is to interpret the Rule, to make the decisions as to its being lived, and to see to it that the monastic life *is* being lived.

St. Benedict says, after his chapter on the qualities of the abbot, "As often as anything important is to be done in the monastery, the abbot shall call the whole community together and himself explain what the business is; and after hearing the advice of the brothers, let him ponder it and follow what he judges the wiser course" (*RB 1980* 3, 1-2). This kind of gathering is not a chapter meeting but what we call today a community meeting, which everyone is eligible to attend. Note that the community only gives advice, it does not make a decision. The abbot has that right and responsibility. He does listen to advice, and he should do this before making important decisions, but the abbot's decision is final.

Since the superior holds the place of Christ and is the spiritual father of the monastery, monks certainly can have recourse to him when they feel that he has given them a job that is beyond their strength or ability. St. Benedict says that an individual with one of these assignments should accept it in obedience, but "should he see, however, that the weight of the burden is altogether too much for his strength, then he should choose the appropriate moment and explain patiently to his superior the reasons why he cannot perform the task. This he ought to do without pride, obstinacy, or refusal. If, after the explanation, the superior is still determined to hold to his original order, then the junior must recognize that this is best for him. Trusting in God's help, he must in love obey" (*RB 1980* 68, 2-5).

He must obey, because he is not obeying the human person, but Christ, whose place the abbot or abbess holds. When I said above that the vow of obedience is to a person I did not mean the human person of this particular superior but the Person of Christ speaking through him or her. We do not see and hear Christ directly but through another who has the leadership role in the community. But this role is simply and only to be Christ to the community and to continue in place and in time Christ's leadership role with regard to his disciples. "He who hears you hears me" (Lk. 10:16; quoted in *RB*, ch. 5, Obedience).

Following this discussion of obedience, let us briefly look at poverty and chastity, which Benedictines traditionally include in the vow of *conversatio*. St. Benedict has discussed them quite well.

Benedictine poverty is not to be deprivation; it is by no means the poverty of St. Francis of Assisi. St. Benedict's guiding principles are common ownership and relative need. Both of these are based on the life of the Jerusalem Church as described in the Acts of the Apostles (4:32-35).

St. Benedict calls personal ownership an "evil practice" which must be "uprooted and removed from the monastery" (*RB 1980* 33, 1). Everything is to be owned in common. What the monk has for his own use has to be either given or permitted by the abbot, and what he has is based on his need. Everyone is not going to have the same needs, so everyone is not going to have the same items. St. Benedict says that there should be on the part of the abbot a "consideration for weaknesses" (*RB 1980* 34, 2); a monk's physical condition is going to demand certain things, and there are mental needs that an abbot has to consider, too.

It is not only a person's weakness that will determine what he should have for his personal use but also his work and, I might add, his mode of recreation. While some might call an individual's mode of recreation a weakness, as if he has to be "humored" in, say, his fondness for listening to classical music, I'm afraid this attitude smacks of the envy St. Benedict doesn't want to exist (*RB 1980* 34, 3-7).

The guide here for the Benedictine is simply what he vowed on his profession day: the monastic life. Each one has to make his own peace with this. So before he asks permission for something for himself he must decide whether or not it's going to be a help in seeking union with God.

In striving for personal poverty, Benedictines must also face the question of communal poverty. When a community puts up an abbey it is built to be permanent. Benedictines build for centuries. (It's a little hard to envision today's buildings lasting for more than fifty years, but that's the general idea.) Since the monastery is a permanent home, from novitiate to cemetery, and since the Holy Rule says it is to be a self-contained little cosmos (*RB*, ch. 4), it can develop into quite a place. Too, Benedictines can be sitting on some rather expensive real estate, but only because they were there long before villages became suburbs. Corporately they can be, and usually are, rather well-to-do. But in today's economy "well-to-do" for all religious means that they are, to use an old depression term, property-poor—they have real estate but no ready cash. So, in spite of appearances, it takes a lot of scrimping, hard work, and even begging, by the monks and nuns, to keep their monasteries operating in the black.

A Benedictine is a disciple who is able to follow Christ with absolute freedom. Because he is totally attached to God he is detached from everything and everyone else. It is the whole idea of singleness of purpose. He may use things because of need, but he has to be detached from them. And, unlike those who are married, he chooses to go to God alone, without the help of someone who would be so much a part of him as to make with him "one flesh."

A monk or nun necessarily has to be celibate. He has a special grace for this. Cenobites have the help of their community, but each one is, after all, one in "one flesh." Does this make them better disciples than those in the married state? By no means. The whole point of discipleship is following Christ alone and totally. The married person has to follow Christ alone but doesn't do so alone. The bond of the cenobite with his community is not the bond of the sacrament of Matrimony, nor does it mean anything comparable.

I shall not repeat what I have already said in Chapter 4 on this subject. By this time the reader knows the function of the vow of chastity and its place in the monastic life. Monks and nuns certainly know already.

*   *   *

Having completed our study of the vows, we will end with two final aspects of the Benedictine way: work and recreation.

As for work, let me simply say that Benedictines should work, that the work should be necessary, and that it must be part of and foster the monastic life and always be subservient to the main work of the community: the *Opus Dei.*

In their choice of work, Benedictines must remember that there is a twofold need: that of the Church and that of the monks and nuns themselves. The need of the Church is obvious, particularly today with the dwindling number of diocesan priests and other religious congregations. But the demands of this work should not be allowed to become a detriment to the monastic life. Monasteries have to do the work that they can do, and the work should be adapted to them. Any work that places too great a burden on the members of the community and causes their spiritual life to suffer, may be beyond their grace of state. Emergency situations may arise which temporarily interfere with monastic regularity, but emergency situations shouldn't become permanent. If they do, something is very wrong.

A mature and seasoned Benedictine will be able to organize both his work and his monastic life without detriment to either. He brings with him his habit of continual prayer, his personal devotions, and his dependence on *lectio divina*. Although there may be times when his work may change his personal schedule, he can probably arrange to pray the *Opus Dei* at the proper times, and certainly should make it his first duty. If he works in an institution outside of the monastery, such as in a hospital or school, the monk can certainly bring his monastic spirituality to those he serves. What a treasurehouse he is able to give them from his experience of the liturgy, the Bible, the great Catholic authors, and Benedictine family living!

Even though Benedictines may be sent out for various tasks, St. Benedict wants his monks to live and work in "the enclosure of the monastery" because being outside in the world "is not at all good for their souls" (*RB 1980* 4, 78). The monk or nun wants God alone, and "the world" does not. By "the world" I mean what Christ meant when he said, "If you were of the world, the world would love its own; but because you are not of the world, but I chose you out of the world, therefore the world hates you" (Jn. 15:19).

"The world," then, is creation divorced by men's minds and wills from God. This is what a person leaves when he comes to the monastery and why it is dangerous for him to go back into it. This is not an "escape mentality," nor entering a monastery merely to "save one's soul." The person's motive is to seek a life of union with God and he can best do this in a God-centered milieu in company with other like-minded people.

For this reason a monk does not seek "the world" as the source of his personal recreation. This does not mean that he may not go out of the monastery for the purpose of recreation, but his excursions should be motivated by his habitual search for God and God's will. This can include such things as a good dinner with friends, a play, a sports event. A Benedictine must have balance, and balance includes recreation for the sake of recreation.

Recreation is both common and personal and I am sure the monks had both at St. Benedict's Monte Cassino. Benedictine commentators on the Rule believe that St. Benedict allowed for periods of talking from what he says about speaking and laughter. Such periods would be brief, or else he would have mentioned them in his arrangement of the day in Chapter 48. But they certainly formed part of the monastic day in practice in our early history.

I have equated common recreation with conversation times because that is what the latter were (and are) supposed to be: times when the monks could get together and communicate with each other for a while as a little break in the day's work.

Common recreation is necessary for good community living. It need not be long, and it may occur only once a day, but all should be present, to give everyone the opportunity of knowing each other well. Here is a time for going out of oneself to the others, of forgetting one's work, the school, the shops, the farm, and realizing the purpose of all these individuals in coming together. It is so easy to get absorbed in one's life and pursuits, and forget that community life is not so much cooperating with each other, as it is living with each other.

Watching television together is not this common recreation. A person watches television because he wants to watch a particular program, or just television in general. The fact that he does so with a group doesn't mean that he is there to communicate. He is there to watch, and he may only communicate during the commercials. No, I'm afraid that television is not a substitute for common recreation. The focal point is the telelvision set, not one's brothers or sisters. Of course there can be a lot of enjoyable give and take by a small group that works together and knows each other well, when watching television. This whole matter is something for the community to talk over.

Television itself may be a good thing for the community, but never too much and never programs that favor the values of "the world." Bringing "the world" into the monastery is something that St. Benedict is totally against: "No one should presume to relate to anyone else what he saw or heard outside the monastery, because that causes the greatest harm. If anyone does so presume, he shall be subjected to the punishment of the rule" (*RB 1980* 67, 4-6).

The way "the world" can get in is through certain types of recreation. For the Benedictine, recreation is edification in the literal sense—building up, never dissipating, what he has already built up. The monk may be having enough trouble in working at continual prayer and finding enough time for real *lectio divina* and other periods of personal prayer. Recreation he needs but he doesn't need the allurements that are going to take him away from his monastic life.

*　　　*　　　*

In conclusion, the Benedictine Way all comes down to the monastic's attitudes—what he values—for where his treasure is, there his heart will be. His daily work is important only because God wills it, and he goes to God in his will. A monk or nun will, then, view work sacramentally, as an outward sign that contains and gives God. Because of this attitude he does not see his work as inimical to a life of union with God but as a necessary means. He will live in an atmosphere of God, of God the Trinity, whose life is giving. He will look forward to *lectio divina*, even if this is possible only in snatches, as a time to be with God with greater attention. The Liturgy of the Eucharist and of the Hours, far from being an interruption and a duty, will be a continuation of his life with God, and a greater union with Christ who is offering his own sacrifice and praise to the Father.

He looks forward to the evening, when he can chat with his community, support and cheer (and be supported and cheered), relax with God, or read an enjoyable book. Benedictines have traditionally turned to night as a good time for praying. After a busy day the idea of praying may not seem relaxing, but true prayer, or to use the monastic term, pure prayer, is. The quiet of the night invites the monk to sit down before God, as David did, and simply be quiet. There is no busy-ness here, not much thinking, just enough to keep attentive and foster desire. He gives himself to God and God gives Himself to him.

A monastery in which each one is truly seeking God and wants God alone, in which each is aware of his or her role in the Church, is going to be the nearest thing to heaven on earth. It will be truly the Blessed City, Jerusalem!

NOTES

[1]Cf. Claude Peifer, OSB, "Monastic Formation and Profession" in *RB 1980*, pp. 457-463.

[2]*Ibid.*, pp. 462-463.

[3]*St. Benedict* (New York: Sheed and Ward, 1937), pp. 147-167. Also as a Doubleday Image Book, 1958, same pages. In a note on p. 166 McCann is quite close to Dom Steidle's conclusion.